Concerning the Affirmation of Divine Oneness

[Risāla fi't-Tawḥīd]

Concerning the Affirmation of Divine Oneness

[Risāla fi'ṭ-Ṭawḥīd]

A TREATISE ON HIDDEN ASSOCIATION [SHIRK KHAFĪ]

SHAIKH WALĪ RASLĀN AD-DIMASHQĪ

WITH THE COMMENTARIES OF

SHAIKH ZAKARIYYĀ' al-ANṢĀRĪ (d. A.H. 926)

and

SHAIKH 'ALĪ b. 'AṬIYYA 'ALAWĀN al-ḤAMAWĪ (d. A.H. 936)

TRANSLATED FROM THE ARABIC BY MUHTAR HOLLAND

AL-BAZ PUBLISHING, INC.
FORT LAUDERDALE, FLORIDA

"And I am not one of those who attribute partners (to Allāh)" Qur'ān (6:79)

Cover Design: Rohana Filippi

Using watercolor and wax to combine the beauty of Arabic script with the Qur'ānic message on paper, Italian artist Rohana Filippi has developed her own artistic style through personal research and inner inspiration. Her art is entirely devoted to "expressing Allāh's presence everywhere."
Ms. Filippi, who currently resides in Canada, has lived and worked in Italy, England, Mexico, and the United States.

Cover Design: Dryden Design, Houston, Texas
Cover Preparation: Designbyindigo.com, Ft. Lauderdale, Florida

Body text set in Jilani and Ghazali fonts by Al-Baz Publishing, Inc.

Printed on acid-free paper.

Library of Congress
Catalog Card Number: 97-74907

ISBN: 978-1-882216-05-5
Concerning the Affirmation of Divine Oneness

First Edition December 1997
Second Edition January 2011

Published by Al-Baz Publishing, Inc.

1516 NE 38th Street, Oakland Park, Florida 33334
Phone: (425) 891-5444 E-mail: albaz@bellsouth.net

Printed and bound in the United States of America by Sheridan Books, Inc.

Contents

PUBLISHER'S PREFACE *vii*

ACKNOWLEDGMENTS *ix*

TRANSLATOR'S INTRODUCTION *xi*

CONCERNING THE AUTHORS *xv*

BOOK ONE
The Risāla fi't-Tawḥīd of Shaikh Walī Raslān ad-Dimashqī **5**

BOOK TWO
The Kitāb Fatḥ ar-Raḥmān of Shaikh Zakariyyā' al-Anṣārī
(Commentary on the *Risāla* of Shaikh Walī Raslān) **11**

BOOK THREE
The Sharḥ Fatḥ ar-Raḥmān of Shaikh ʿAlī ibn ʿAṭiyya ʿAlawān al-Ḥamawī
(Commentary on the *Risāla* of Shaikh Walī Raslān) **37**

ABOUT THE TRANSLATOR **103**

Publisher's Preface

It is convenient to call this page the 'Publisher's Preface', but in truth, I am not really a publisher. In a certain outer sense it is true that I am, for if I were not, this book would never have reached you.

The reality is, however, that I am a miner, and I mine the sands of time to find the gold that is buried in the scholarly repositories of Arabic and Persian manuscripts around the world; the works of those blessed saintly friends of Allāh, the *awliyā*ʾ, who have reached the other shore and met their souls' desire, yet for His sake have turned back to offer their hand to those who might drown if they did not. Shaikh Walī Raslān was one such *walī,* and what is presented here, in this volume, is his hand stretched out to you, dear reader.

Walī Raslān's *Risāla,* to put it rather graphically, is a lot of meat in a little sandwich. It gets to the heart of the matter without any delay and stays there for a full five pages. After reading it and reading the two commentaries, you will be left with no illusions about your own abilities to attain to beloved Allāh. So what then, dear brother or sister? This business of ours, if we want to call it that, has four stages; the *Sharīʿa*, the *Ṭarīqa*, the *Ḥaqīqa* and the *Maʿrifa.* The first two are the uttermost boundary that we can reach by means of our own striving. Thereafter it depends upon the grace of Allāh to His creature. What ***is*** the *Ḥaqīqa*? Is it a further kind of teaching to which one graduates after long years of progress in the *Ṭarīqa*? The answer to that question, is that no, it isn't. The *Ḥaqīqa* is the living grace of the All-Merciful, and He bestows it upon whom He wills of His creatures.

Reader, if you can, try to find your way to the *Ḥaqīqa*, for it is the pearl beyond price. Look for someone that can pass on the contact or give you the opening, because it is very seldom that it is bestowed directly, no matter how ardently one may long for it, or pray for it.

A word of caution: If ever you are told that the opening depends on effort of your own, or visualizing certain symbols or words, or certain prayers, or fasting; know that you are not in the presence of one who has been opened to the *Ḥaqīqa*. The opening is a simple matter and the contact with the *Ḥaqīqa* is passed on from one who has already been opened, by permission of Allāh. The *Ḥaqīqa* is always there, and it always was, the whole of your life; what veils you from it is the *nafs*, that useful servant given us by Allāh (Exalted is He) to serve our needs during our sojourn in this world. When that veil is pierced, we are able to receive for ourselves the direct experience of guidance for our lives, both inwardly and outwardly, in a way that carries its own proof, and all that remains is to live one's life with care. Not that the *Ḥaqīqa* replaces religion; rather it provides a content for it, and the prayers become a delight, accompanied as they are by the One to whom they are addressed.

May the Lord of all the worlds guide you to all that is good and open up your way to Him. *Āmīn*, dear reader!

Ruslan Moore
October 1997

Acknowledgments

All praise is due to Allāh, the Beneficent, the Merciful!

We bear witness that there is no god except Allāh, and that Muḥammad is the Messenger of Allāh!

Our Lord, thank You for giving us this wholesome task!

Grateful thanks to Muhtar Holland for devoting years of his life to translating these works; may Allāh bless him! Grateful thanks to my mother Liza for her unstinting love and support down the years. We would like especially to thank and recognize G. W. J. Drewes for his scholarly work entitled, "*Directions for Travellers on the Mystic Path*: Zakariyyā' al-Anṣarī's *Kitāb Fatḥ al-Raḥman* and its Indonesian adaptations." Thanks also to the many who have helped make this publication possible, among them the following:

The Library of the University of Leiden
Ridwan Lowther for research
Rohana Filippi for the cover art

Translator's Introduction

Of the introductory material I have to offer in this volume, a major portion is presented in the separate section headed "Concerning the Authors." I trust that the following points will also be of interest, and helpful to the reader:

Concerning Shaikh Walī Raslān's *Risāla.*

From all we know of Shaikh Walī Raslān's everyday life, extravagance of any kind was totally alien to him. He was certainly not one to squander either the spoken or the written word. Even as the charismatic spiritual teacher depicted in traditional tales, we find him working wonders of demonstration, while adding only a few sentences of verbal explanation. In the literary sphere, he is said to have written at least one poem, expressing his praise of the Lord, and a few of his brief spontaneous utterances *[shadharāt]* have been recorded. In his most precious legacy, the *Risāla*, not a single word could possibly be considered redundant. The work covers barely five pages in my English translation, which is inevitably less concise than the original.

In exercising his preference for terse expression, the saintly Shaikh was aided by the linguistic structure of his native tongue. In Arabic, the subject of his brief but powerful treatise is summed up in the single word *tawḥīd*. This term is derived from the three-consonant root *w–ḥ–d*, which serves as the vehicle for the basic concept of "oneness," or "unity," along with the closely related ideas of "singularity" and "uniqueness." These root letters are clearly apparent in the numerical adjective *wāḥid* [one]. In the words of the Qur'ān:

Your God is surely One. (37:4) *inna Ilāha-kum la-Wāḥid.*

This is undoubtedly the central message of the Book of Allāh (Almighty and Glorious is He), and it is repeated in many other verses *[āyāt]*. If a believer in that message is the subject of the verb *waḥḥada*, it tells us that he affirmed the Divine Oneness, by making a statement like: "My God is surely One." With similar economy, the verbal noun *tawḥīd* is enough to describe that profession of belief, and it can therefore be translated as "the-affirmation-of-Oneness." (The use of hyphens is not strictly necessary, of course, but it may help to remind us that the author of the *Risāla* employs the single word *tawḥīd*.)

The opposite of *tawḥīd* is expressed by the Arabic term *shirk*, derived from the root *sh–r–k*, which conveys the notion of "sharing" or "partnership." The word *sharīk* (plural *shurakāʾ*) means "partner" or "associate." In the words of the Qurʿān:

Say: "My prayer and my sacrifice,	*qul inna ṣalātī wa nusukī*
and my living and my dying are for	*wa maḥyāya wa mamātī*
Allāh, the Lord of All the Worlds.	*li'llāhi Rabbi 'l-ʿālamīn:*
He has no partner." (6:162,163)	*lā sharīka la-h.*

The term *shirk* means "associating partners with Allāh," and the related term *mushrik* is applied to someone guilty of such polytheistic association. Shaikh Walī Raslān lived during the time of the Crusades, and his hometown of Damascus was seldom far removed from the conflicts that raged throughout that era. The Crusaders championed a particular form of *shirk*, the doctrine of the Trinity, which the Qurʾān explicitly refutes:

O People of the Book...,	*yā Ahla 'l-Kitābi...*
believe in Allāh	*āminū bi'llāhi*
and His Messengers,	*wa Rusuli-h:*
and do not say "Three"....	*wa lā taqūlū thalātha...*
Allāh is only One God. (4:171)	*inna-ma 'llāhu Ilāhun Wāḥid.*

By some accounts, the Shaikh was active as a warrior-saint, and he may well have been physically involved in the defence of Damascus, when the city came under direct assault. He was certainly an active opponent of all blatant, overt forms of *shirk*. In his *Risāla*, however, his defence of *tawḥīd* is aimed at a more subtle target, the spiritual defect called *shirk khafī* [hidden, or covert, association of partners with Allāh, the One and Only God]. As used by Shaikh Walī Raslān, the term *tawḥīd* may therefore demand an even lengthier translation, namely: "the *realization*-and-affirmation-of-Oneness."

Concerning the Commentaries on the *Risāla*.

Without suggesting that Shaikh Walī Raslān has not essentially "said it all" in his own inimitable style, I feel sure that the reader will welcome the commentaries of Shaikh Zakariyyā᾿ al-Anṣārī and Shaikh ʿAlī ibn ʿAṭiyya ʿAlawān al-Ḥamawī.[1] The task of translating the *Risāla* would have been daunting indeed, had I not enjoyed the benefit of their wise and insightful observations. As a further advantage, the commentators refer quite frequently to variant readings in the *Risāla* manuscripts at their disposal. If only indirectly, this gave me access to several extra copies of Shaikh Walī Raslān's treatise, copies that are otherwise unobtainable, and possibly no longer in existence.

Apart from their own explanatory value, these commentaries contain one truly vital asset: the complete text of the *Risāla* itself. Though the words of Shaikh Walī Raslān are not presented as a continuous text, but interspersed throughout the commentaries, they are clearly distinguished by traditional manuscript techniques. In the work of Shaikh Zakariyyā᾿, the explanations are often inserted between separate words and phrases, whereas Shaikh ʿAlī usually quotes a sentence from the *Risāla* intact, then follows it with a passage of his own. Such differences are immediately apparent in the translated versions, where the words and sentences from the *Risāla* have been printed in a bold font.

There is one puzzling question, to which no satisfactory answer can be offered at present, concerning the titles of the two commentaries. Can it be by sheer coincidence, that each is entitled *Fatḥ ar-Raḥmān* [Inspiration of the All-Merciful], the only difference being that one is called the *Kitāb* [Book] thereof, whereas the other is named the *Sharḥ* [Commentary]? Both are unmistakably direct commentaries on the *Risāla*, and there is no evidence to support the notion that *Sharḥ Fatḥ ar-Raḥmān* might be an indirect commentary on Shaikh Walī Raslān's work, based on *Kitāb Fatḥ ar-Raḥmān*.

[1] It should be noted that Brockelmann, in his *Geschichte der arabischen Literatur*, lists no fewer than seven commentaries on the *Risāla*.

A concluding invocation.

I feel moved to close this introduction by quoting the words of Allāh (Almighty and Glorious is He), addressed to His Messenger Muḥammad (Allāh bless him and give him peace):

Say: "I am only a mortal like you.	*qul inna-mā ana basharun*
It is revealed to me	*mithlu-kum yūḥā ilayya*
that your God	*anna-mā Ilāhu-kum*
is One God,	*Ilāhun Wāḥid:*
so whoever hopes	*fa-man kāna yarjū*
for the meeting with his Lord,	*liqā'a Rabbi-hi*
let him do righteous work,	*fa-l'-ya'mal*
and let him give no one	*'amalan ṣāliḥan*
any share at all	*wa lā yushrik*
in the worship	*bi-'ibādati*
due unto his Lord." (18:110)	*Rabbi-hi aḥadā.*

Allāh (Exalted is He) has also assured his servants that:

Your God is One God.	*wa Ilāhu-kum*
There is no god but He,	*Ilāhun Wāḥid:*
the All-Merciful,	*lā ilāha illā*
the All-Compassionate. (2:163)	*Huwa 'r-Raḥmānu 'r-Raḥīm.*

May the One and Only God, Allāh, have mercy on us all, and treat us with compassion! *Āmīn.*

Muhtar Holland
September 1997

Concerning the Authors

1. Shaikh Walī Raslān ad-Dimashqī

Where did Shaikh Walī Raslān spend most of his earthly life, including his final moments? As indicated by his universally accepted surname, ad-Dimashqī, the undisputed answer to this question is the Syrian city of Damascus. But when did he live there, and in what year did he die? That is harder to answer with absolute certainty, since the Arabic sources give a wide range of dates for his death: from shortly after A.H. 540/1145 C.E., to A.H. 695/1296 C.E., to as late as A.H. 711/1369 C.E. After venturing into the maze of conflicting sources, the Dutch scholar G. W. J. Drewes emerges with the convincing conclusion that the earliest of these dates is most probably correct.

In one later compilation, Drewes notes, "A.H. 461 as the year of Raslān's birth is given without mention of the source of this information." As indicated by another of his surnames, al-Jaʿbarī, his actual birthplace was the fort of Qalʿat Jaʿbar, on the left bank of the Euphrates, where his male relatives were members of a militia formation known as the *ajnād*. Those were the days of the Crusades, so the threat of invasion by the Franks may well have prompted the family to make their move to the Muslim stronghold of Damascus. Yet another of the Shaikh's surnames is "the Carpenter *[an-Nashshār]*." According to traditional accounts, he worked at the carpenter's trade for twenty years, before embarking on his remarkable spiritual career. The turning point came when his own saw told him that sawing wood was not his true purpose in life; after two unsuccessful attempts, it finally won his attention by breaking into three pieces. Raslān then became a pupil of Abū ʿĀmir al-Muʾaddib, a Ṣūfī Shaikh whose *silsila* [spiritual pedigree] linked him to Sari as-Saqati, the uncle and teacher of the celebrated al-Junaid.[1]

[1] See note 71 on p. 74 below.

As Drewes tells the story:

"To this master he made over his earnings, in exchange for which Abū ʿĀmir supplied his meals, not however without his going hungry from time to time.... His habitation was of the simplest: nothing but a lean-to beside the workshop he shared with a weaver. Abū ʿĀmir's tuition took place in a small mosque in the neighborhood, within the Thomas Gate..., a district inhabited from of old by many Christians. This mosque, to this very day, [is] known by the name of Maqām Shaikh Arslān...."[2]

When Abū ʿĀmir died, Raslān the Carpenter became Raslān the Shaikh, for his teacher had chosen him as his successor, preferring him over his own son. Shaikh Raslān's way of life remained extremely simple, and he never married. Through his steadfast devotion to the Truth, he came to be widely known as Walī Raslān, meaning Raslān the Saint.

Many charismatic powers and supernatural talents have been attributed to Shaikh Walī Raslān, including those related in *Qalāʾid al-Jawāhir [Necklaces of Gems]*. In this work, which is essentially a biography of Shaikh ʿAbd al-Qādir al-Jīlānī (may Allāh be well pleased with him), Shaikh Muḥammad ibn Yaḥyā at-Tādifī includes the following section:

Shaikh Raslān ad-Dimashqī

One of the leading Shaikhs who paid glowing tribute to him [Shaikh ʿAbd al-Qādir al-Jīlānī (may Allāh be well pleased with him)] was that splendid exemplar, Shaikh Raslān ad-Dimashqī (may Allāh be well pleased with him).

He was one of the pre-eminent Shaikhs of Syria, one of those remarkable individuals who know through direct experience *[aʿyān al-ʿārifīn]*, and one of those who are outstanding on account of their superior skills. He was endowed with lofty indications, with elevated aspirations, with truthful expressions, with supernatural charismatic exploits *[karāmāt khāriqa]*, with majestic spiritual stations, and with

[2] The name Raslān is probably an arabicized form of Arslān, which is the Turkish word for "lion," also used metaphorically in the sense of "brave man." It also appears in the Persian dictionary (marked as being of Turkish origin) with a note that it was adopted as a title by many Persian kings.

exalted situations. He held the highest degree of directly acquired forms of knowledge *[maʿārif]*, the loftiest position in the realm of the realities *[ḥaqāʾiq]*, and the foremost standing in nearness, clear unveiling and brilliant illumination *[fatḥ]*, as well as a firmly established empowerment and an effective aptitude for management.

He is one of the leading figures of this [spiritual] business, and one of its pillars, in terms of learning *[ʿilm]* and practice *[ʿamal]*, real achievement *[taḥqīq]*, direct knowledge *[maʿrifa]*, and indifference to worldly concerns *[zuhd]*. He is one of those whom Allāh (Exalted is He) has brought to the notice of his fellow creatures, and upon whom He has conferred acceptance and abundant veneration in their sight. He put him in firm possession of the spiritual states *[aḥwāl]* and of sainthood *[wilāya]*, made him privy to the mysteries of the universe *[asrār al-kawn]*, and granted him freedom of disposal in the realm of existence *[wujūd]*. At his hands, He manifested wondrous marvels, for his sake He disrupted the customary patterns of nature, and He appointed him as a leader *[imām]* for the spiritual travelers *[sālikīn]*.

He eventually became responsible for the training of all the seekers *[murīdīn]* in Syria. A group of its Shaikhs became affiliated with him, and not a few of its inhabitants enjoyed the benefit of his fellowship. The religious scholars *[ʿulamāʾ]* and the elders (may Allāh be well pleased with them) pointed him out with profound respect and reverent admiration. Various animals used for transport alighted in his courtyard, arriving from every direction and by every route, and riders followed in his tracks from every deep ravine *[min kulli fajjin ʿamīq]*.[3]

Shaikh Raslān ad-Dimashqī (may Allāh be well pleased with him) was charming, graceful, courteous and humble. He combined the most noble traits of character, the most perfect manners, and the most excellent attributes. He was also endowed with a sublime way of speaking about the process of real experiences *[minhāj al-ḥaqāʾiq]*.

He explained, for instance, that one who knows by experience *[al-ʿārif]* is closely monitored in everything by his direct vision *[mushāhada]*, and that intimate knowledge *[maʿrifa]* becomes manifest in the revelation of insight. This is because one who knows by direct experience has already reached his spiritual destination *[al-ʿārif wāṣil]*,

[3] An allusion to Q. 22:27.

but then the secrets of Allāh (Exalted is He) are conveyed to him in a complete totality, by the lights that make him privy to the facts of the unseen *[shawāhid al-ghaib]*, and privy to the secret of control. Thus he is taken from his own person *[nafs]*, then restored to his own person, firmly established in his heart. His being taken from his own person is an act of bringing near [to the Lord], while his being restored to his own person is a training exercise *[tahdhīb]*, and his self-control is a special assignment *[takhṣīṣ]*. The bringing near *[taqrīb]* causes him to witness, the training causes him to exist, and the special assignment gives him a separate identity. Thus his separate identity *[tafrīd]* is his existence *[wujūd]*, his existence is his witnessing *[shuhūd]*, and his witnessing is his witnessing. As Allāh (Exalted is He) has told us:

The eyes do not perceive Him,	*lā tudriku-hu 'l-abṣāru*
but He perceives the eyes. (6:104)	*wa Huwa yudriku 'l-abṣār.*

—so His perceiving of the eyes is witnessed by the faculties of insight *[baṣā'ir]*.

It was the enlightened Shaikh Abū Muḥammad Ibrāhīm ibn Maḥmūd al-Ya'lī who said:

"One day in the springtime, Shaikh Raslān (may Allāh be well pleased with him) was in one of the gardens of Damascus, together with a group of his companions. One of them said to him: 'O my master, what is the saint *[walī]* who is fully endowed with the principles of enablement *[aḥkām at-tamkīn]*.' 'My dear young son,' he replied, 'he is the one whom Allāh (Exalted is He) has invested with the reins of management *[taṣrīf]*.' His companion then asked: 'What is the distinctive mark of that condition, O my master?'

"The Shaikh responded by picking up four twigs. He singled out one of them and said: 'This twig represents the summer. He singled out another and said: 'This twig stands for the fall, the autumn season.' He singled out another and said: 'This one represents the winter.' Then he singled out yet another and said: 'This one stands for the spring.' He then took the twig which he had designated for the summer, and waved it to and fro with his hand. As he did so, the weather grew intensely hot. Then he threw that twig away, picked out the one he had designated for the fall or autumn, and waved it to and fro. As he did so, along came all the typical features of autumn and the season of the fall. Then he threw that twig away, picked out the one he had designated for the winter, and waved it to and fro. As he did so, the winter winds began to blow, the weather grew bitterly cold, and then the leaves began to wither on the trees in the garden, and so on. Then he threw that twig away, held onto the one he had designated for the spring, and waved it to and fro. As he did so, the trees turned green with fresh leaves, the branches began to blossom, and the breezes of springtime blew.

"Then he gazed at the birds on the trees in the garden. He went over to one of the trees, gave it a shake, and signaled to the bird perched on it: 'Glorify your Creator!' The bird responded by warbling a most lovely tune, filling the listeners with sheer delight. Then he moved over to another tree, and did the same again, and so on, until he had come to each of the trees. Of all the birds, only one had failed to break into song, so the Shaikh (may Allāh be well pleased with him) said to it: 'May you not stay alive!'—and it promptly fell dead on the ground."

On another occasion, fifteen men came to visit him, but the only food he had in store consisted of five flat loaves of bread. He set these before them, after crumbling them with careful precision, and said: "In the Name of Allāh, the All-Merciful, the All-Compassionate. O Allāh, bless us in what you have provided for us, for You are the Best of providers!" Even when they had eaten till their hunger was fully satisfied, a quantity was still left over, so he divided it amongst them, piece by piece, and they traveled on to Baghdād, eating from it throughout the entire length of their journey.

It was Abū Aḥmad ibn Muḥammad al-Kurdī who said: "I once saw the Shaikh (may Allāh be well pleased with him) traveling through the air. At one time he would be walking, at one time he would be traveling in a cross-legged posture, at one time he would be flying by like an arrow, and at one time he would be passing over the water."

He went on to say: "I also saw him at ʿArafāt, and at all the sacred shrines *[mashāʿir]*. Then I lost sight of him, so when I came to Damascus I asked the people of that city about him, and they told me: 'By Allāh, he has not been absent from us for as much as one whole day, except on the Day of ʿArafa, part of the Day of Sacrifice *[Yawm an-Naḥr]*, and the Days of *Tashrīq*.'"

He also said: "I saw him sitting one day with a lion snuggled against his feet, but he was too absorbed to take the slightest notice of the lion.

"One day I saw him on the outskirts of Damascus, throwing pebbles, so I asked him to explain, and he said: 'These are arrows, aimed at the Franks.' At that very point in time, the Franks had moved out toward the coast, pursued by an army of the Muslims. Shortly after that, people said: 'We saw pebbles descending from the sky, raining down through the air upon the heads of the Franks.' A large number of them perished because of the stones cast by the Shaikh. It even happened that a single pebble would strike a mounted knight, and he and his horse would both be destroyed, through the grace of the Shaikh (may Allāh be well pleased with him)."

He was resident (may Allāh be well pleased with him) in Damascus, which he regarded as his home town, and it was there that he died. He was buried on its outskirts, and his tomb is a conspicuous site, regularly visited down to this day of ours.[4] While his bier was being carried on the necks of the bearers, green birds attended and perched on his bier. The people also saw cavaliers mounted on gray horses, circling around the funeral procession. They had never seen them before, nor did they ever see them afterwards.

May Allāh be well pleased with him!

2. Shaikh Zakariyyā᾿ al-Anṣārī

There is no shortage of information concerning the author of *Kitāb Fatḥ ar-Raḥmān [Book of the Inspiration of the All-Merciful]*, a commentary on the *Risāla* of Shaikh Walī Raslān. We know that Shaikh Zakariyyā᾿ al-Anṣārī died in Cairo in A.H. 926/1520 C.E., having lived for a full hundred years. As a renowned exponent of the Shāfiʿī school of Islamic jurisprudence *[fiqh]*, he acquired the honorary title of *Shaikh*

[4] The author of *Qalā᾿id al-Jawāhir [Necklaces of Gems]* died in A.H. 963/1556 C.E., so more than four centuries have elapsed since the time he calls "this day of ours." Even in our own day, however, Drewes assures us that Shaikh Wali Raslān's mausoleum, "flanked by the tombs of his master and his servant, is to be found in the cemetery named after him outside the Thomas Gate [in Damascus]."

al-Islām. His fame is widespread in the Islamic world, and his works have attracted particular attention in Indonesia and Malaysia.

Shaikh Zakariyyā' al-Anṣārī has not been neglected by Western scholars. He is discussed by J. Schacht in the *Encyclopaedia of Islam*, in the course of an article on ash-Sha'rānī, a pupil of Zakariyyā' who described his master as a "pillar of Islamic jurisprudence *[fiqh]* and spiritual culture *[taṣawwuf]*." He is mentioned by J. S. Trimingham,[5] as the author of *al-Futūḥāt al-Ilāhiyya [The Divine Revelatory Disclosures]*. In Brockelmann's *History of Islamic Literature*, no fewer than fifty-two titles are listed under his name, covering subjects such as logic, grammar, scientific terminology, rhetoric, prosody, Qur'anic exegesis *[tafsīr]*, Sacred Tradition *[Ḥadīth Qudsī]*, the life of the Prophet (Allāh bless him and give him peace), several topics of jurisprudence *[fiqh]*, theological doctrine *[kalām]* and spiritual culture *[taṣawwuf]*.

Most importantly, we have the excellent scholarly work of G. W. J. Drewes, whose *Directions for Travellers on the Mystic Path* bears the subtitle: "Zakariyyā' al-Anṣārī's *Kitāb Fatḥ ar-Raḥmān* and its Indonesian Adaptations." This book contains highly informative chapters on Shaikh Walī Raslān ad-Dimashqī and Shaikh Zakariyyā' al-Anṣārī, as well as a romanized transliteration of the entire text of *Kitāb Fatḥ ar-Raḥmān*.

3. Shaikh 'Alī ibn 'Aṭiyya 'Alawān al-Ḥamawī

As for the author of *Sharḥ Fatḥ ar-Raḥmān*, our second commentary on the *Risāla* of Shaikh Walī Raslān, we have only the scantiest information to offer the reader. We can merely state that his name is 'Alī ibn 'Aṭiyya 'Alawān al-Ḥamawī,[6] that he died in A.H. 939/1530 C.E., and that his work became known in Indonesia. However late in the day, the quality of his work entitles him to wider recognition.

May Allāh be well pleased with each of these three servants of His (Exalted is He).

[5] In *The Sufi Orders in Islam*. Oxford University Press; London, 1971; p. 186. (Trimingham gives A.H. 916/1510 C.E. as the date of Shaikh Zakariyyā' al-Anṣārī's death.)

[6] The surname "al-Ḥamawī" indicates that he lived in the Syrian town of Ḥamā.

Concerning the Affirmation of Divine Oneness

[Risāla fi'ṭ-Ṭawḥīd]

Whatever mercy Allāh opens for mankind,
none can withhold it.
(Qur'ān 35:2)

The *Risāla* of Shaikh Walī Raslān

In the Name of Allāh, the All-Merciful, the All-Compassionate

Praise be to Allāh.

Now then, know that the whole of you is covert polytheism *[shirkun khafiyyun]* and your realization-and-affirmation-of-Oneness *[tawḥīd]* will not become evident to you until you exit from you[rself].

Provided you are sincere, it will be disclosed to you that it is He, not you, so you must ask forgiveness for you. And whenever you encounter [any form of it], your own polytheism *[shirk]* will be evident to you. You must therefore renew, in every hour and at every moment, an affirmation-of-Oneness *[tawḥīd]* and a faith *[īmān]*. And whenever you become detached from them your faith will increase; and whenever you become detached from you, your certitude *[yaqīn]* will increase.

O prisoner of desires and formal acts of worship, O prisoner of stations and revelations! You are deluded and you are preoccupied with you. Where is your preoccupation with Him to the exclusion of you? He is Present and Attentive, "and He is with you wherever you may be," in this world and the hereafter. When you are with Him, He screens you from you, and when you are with you, He screens you from Him.

Faith is your separating from them, and certitude is your separating from you. When your faith has increased, you will be transported from state to state; and when your certitude has increased, you will be transported from station to station.

The Sacred Law *[Sharīʿa]* is for you, until you seek Him from Him for you; and the Reality *[Ḥaqīqa]* belongs to Him, until you seek Him through Him for Him, beyond when and beyond where, for the

Sacred Law does have limits *[ḥudūd]* and modes *[jihāt]*, but the Reality has neither limit nor mode.

One who lives with the Sacred Law [alone] is given the privilege of striving *[mujāhada]* and one who lives with the Reality is given the privilege of grace *[minna]*. How great is the contrast between striving and grace!

One who lives with striving is existent *[mawjūd]*, while one who lives with grace is extinct *[mafqūd]*.

Practices are linked to the noble Law *[Sharʿ]*. As for total trust in the Lord *[tawakkul]*, this is linked to faith *[īmān]*, and the realization-and-affirmation-of-Oneness *[tawḥīd]* is linked to illuminating disclosure *[kashf]*.

People wander astray from the Lord of Truth because of the mind, and from the hereafter because of passion. For, when you seek the Lord of Truth with the mind, you lose the way, and when you seek the hereafter with passion, you stumble and slip.

The believer sees by the light of Allāh, and one who has direct knowledge *[al-ʿārif]* beholds Him by it.

"As long as you are with you, We command you. Then, once you have been rendered extinct to you, We take charge of you." For He does not take charge of them until after their annihilation [in Him].

As long as you continue, you are a seeker *[murīd]*. Then, when He has made you extinct to you, you are one who is sought *[murād]*.

The most lasting certainty is your absence from you and your presence with Him. What a big difference there is between what is at His command and what is because of Him! If you are at His command, worldly means will be subservient to you. And if you are because of Him, the whole universe will be submissive to you.

The first of the stations is patience in obedience to His will (Exalted is He). The one in the middle is contentment with His wishes (Exalted is He), and the last is that you come to be in accordance with His purpose.

[Practical] knowledge *[ʿilm]* is the way of action, and action is [the way of] knowledge. And knowledge is the way of experience *[maʿrifa]*. And experience [of Allāh] is the way of unveiling *[kashf]*. And unveiling is the way of extinction *[fanāʾ]*.

"You have not become fit for Us as long as there is still within you any remnant of anything apart from Us, so when you have set everything else aside, We shall render you extinct. You have now become fit for Us, and We have entrusted you with Our secret."

When there does not remain with you any self-motivation, your certitude will be perfected, and when there does not remain any existence of yours, your realization-and-affirmation-of-Oneness *[tawḥīd]* will be perfected.

The people of the inner are with certainty *[yaqīn]*, and the people of the outer are with faith *[īmān]*. So when the heart of the master of certainty is stimulated in response to anything other than Allāh, his certainty is deficient, and when no notion ever occurs to him, his certainty is perfect. And when the heart of the master of faith is stimulated in response to anything other than the divine command, his faith is defective, and when it is stirred by the divine command, his faith is complete.

The sin of the people of certainty is unbelief *[kufr]*, and the sin of the people of faith is falling short.

The dutiful servant is diligent, and the lover is totally trusting, and he who knows by direct experience *[al-ʿārif]* is calm and serene, and he who is found is lost. There is no rest for a dutiful servant, and no movement for a lover, and no resolve for one who knows by direct experience, and no being found for one who is lost.

Love is experienced only after certainty, and when the lover is sincere in his love, his heart must be empty of all that is apart from Him. And as long as it retains any trace of love for anything but Him, he must be lacking in love.

One who takes delight in misfortune, co-exists therewith, and one who takes delight and rejoices in prosperity co-exists with it, so when He makes them extinct to them, the enjoyment of misfortune and prosperity departs.

As for the lover, his breath is wisdom *[ḥikma]*, and as for the loved one, his breath is power *[qudra]*.

Formal acts of worship are for the compensations, and love is for the nearnesses. [In the words of Allāh (Almighty and Glorious is He)]: "I have prepared for My righteous servants that which no eye has ever seen, of which no ear has ever heard, and which has never occurred to any human heart. When they wish for Me, I give them that which no eye has ever seen and of which no ear has ever heard."

When He has made you extinct to your passion by decree, and to your self-will through knowledge, you will become a servant with undivided loyalty, with neither passion nor will of your own. Then the veil will be lifted for your benefit, so that servitude will vanish away into Oneness, for the servant will be annihilated and the Lord (Almighty and Glorious is He) will remain.

The whole of the Sacred Law *[Sharīʿa]* is constriction, and the whole of knowledge *[ʿilm]* is expansion, and the whole of direct experience *[maʿrifa]* is dalliance and playful teasing.

Our method is love, not labor, and annihilation, not perpetuity. When you enter into work, you belong to you, and when you enter into love, you belong to Him. The worshipper looks to his worship, while the lover looks to his love.

When you have come to acknowledge Him, your breathing will be through Him, and your movements will belong to Him, but if you are ignorant of Him, your movements will be your own.

The formal worshipper *[ʿābid]* has no rest; and the ascetic *[zāhid]* has no appetite; and the champion of truth *[ṣiddīq]* has no dependent reliance; and he who is endowed with direct experience *[ʿārif]* has neither might nor strength, neither choice nor will, neither movement nor rest; and he who is existent *[mawjūd]* has no existence.

When you have come to be on familiar terms with Him, you will be estranged from you.

"If someone is preoccupied with Us for his own sake, We shall make him blind. But if someone is preoccupied with Us for Our sake, We shall give him sight."

When your passion has faded away, the door of the Reality *[Ḥaqīqa]* will be unveiled for your benefit, so that your own will is annihilated and Oneness *[Waḥdāniyya]* is unveiled to you and then you will realize that it is He, not you.

If you surrender to Him, He will draw you close, but if you argue with Him, He will keep you at a distance.

If you draw near through Him, He will bring you close, but if you draw near through you, He will keep you at a distance.

If you seek Him for your own sake, He will burden you, but if you seek Him for His sake, He will pamper you.

Your nearness to Him is your separation from you, while your distance is your sticking with you.

If you come without you, He will accept you, but if you come through you, He will exclude you.

The worker is hardly likely to be free of attachment to his labor. So be one of the sort disposed toward grace *[minna]*, not one of the sort disposed toward work *[ʿamal]*.

If you know Him, you will come to rest, but if you are ignorant of Him, you will be agitated. So the point is that He should be and you should not be.

As for the common folk, their works are suspect, and as for the élite, their works are good deeds, and as for the élite of the élite, their works are degrees of spiritual progress.

Whenever you shun your passion, your faith is reinforced, and whenever you shun your own essence, your realization-and-affirmation-of-Oneness *[tawḥīd]* is reinforced.

Creatures are a screen and you are a screen, but the Lord of Truth is not one to be secluded, and He is concealed from you because of you, and you are concealed from you because of you. So separate from you, and you shall witness Him.

Kitāb Fatḥ ar-Raḥmān

(The Book of the Inspiration of the All-Merciful)

Commentary on the *Risāla* of Walī Raslān[1]

by

Zakariyyā' al-Anṣārī

(d. A.H. 926/1520 C.E.)

[1] In this translation of *Kitāb Fatḥ ar-Raḥmān*, words that occur in the text of the *Risāla* of Walī Raslān are printed in bold font.

In the Name of Allāh
the All-Merciful and Compassionate.

In Him is my trust. May Allāh bless our master Muḥammad, his family and his companions, and give them peace.

These are the words of our chief and master, Shaikh of the Shaikhs of Islām and of the Muslims, adornment of the religion and the faith, Abū Yaḥyā Zakariyyā᾿ al-Anṣārī ash-Shāfi῾ī. May Allāh have mercy on him, and let us continue to enjoy His support in this world and the hereafter through Muḥammad and his family. Surely He is capable of whatever He wills, and competent to answer prayers.

In the name of Allāh, the All-Merciful and Compassionate. Praise be to Him who reserves Uniqueness to Himself and glories in the properties of Lordship, and blessing and peace upon the Prophet and his companions and upon his family and his followers.

Now then, the science of Divine Unity is one of the most noble of the sciences, nay, it is the noblest of them all, and works composed on the subject include *ar-Risāla ar-Raslāniyya*, by the Imām versed in knowledge of Allāh (Exalted is He), Raslān ad-Dimashqī [the Damascene] —may Allāh perfume his resting place and make Paradise his habitation.

Since this is one of the most original books ever written on the science of Divine Unity [*῾ilm at-tawḥīd*], and the most comprehensive treatment of the subject within such a short space, I prayed to Allāh (Exalted is He) for help and guidance in composing a commentary that would analyze its wording and explain its meaning,

and I named my work:

"The Inspiration of the All-Merciful: Commentary on the *Risāla* of Walī Raslān."

Know that knowledge of Divine Unity is called for. Allāh (Exalted is He) has said: "So know that there is none worthy of worship but Allāh," (47:19) thereby necessitating the abolition of polytheistic association *[shirk]*, of which there are two kinds:

1. The outer, manifest kind, which has been discussed and classified by al-Ghazāli and others;

2. The inner, hidden kind, namely the soul's latching onto [worldly] entities, which then form an obstacle to receiving succor from the realm of the Unseen *[ʿālam al-ghaib]*. This amounts to hidden polytheism because it ties one to sensory perceptions, far from the Presence of Holiness *[ḥaḍrat al-quds]*. The author refers to this when he says: **The whole of you,** O servant, in essence *[dhāt]* and attributes *[ṣifāt]* and action *[fiʿl]*, **is [hidden] polytheism,** the source of delusion and fantasy, for these two establish the other [ephemera], such as transitory ranks and stations. So when you make all 'the other' cease to exist as far as you are concerned, there emerges through Divine Knowledge your realization-of-Oneness *[tawḥīd]*, abolishing polytheism in both its forms, necessitating the banishment of delusion and fantasy.

And your realization-of-Oneness does not become evident to you, that is, apparent to you, **until you exit from**—that is, become extinct to—**yourself** and all other things, through your seeing them all as from Allāh (Exalted is He). "But Allāh has created you and your handiwork!" (37:96). The relationship of your deeds to yourself is 'acquisitional,' and to Allāh (Exalted is He) 'creational,' because Allāh (Exalted is He) creates, while you are acquiring *[kāsib]* so as to be rewarded or punished.

Provided you are sincere in making your exit therefrom, **it will be disclosed to you that it is He** (Exalted is He) who is the existent doer, **not you.** Then, when you witness nothing other than Him (Exalted is He), you will become one who experiences His Oneness as a reality. This witnessing may be prolonged, although this is rare, or it may be like a flash of lightning. When this has been revealed to you, **you must ask forgiveness for you,** that is, for your witnessing, because through your deliverance from this the knowledge of *Tawḥīd* will be disclosed to you in respect of essence, attributes and action. **And whenever you encounter any form of it, your own polytheism will be evident to you,** as opposed to what you ascribe to people. **You must therefore renew, in every hour and at every moment,** indeed at every breath, **an affirmation-of-Oneness** that He is the existent doer, **and a faith,** that is, a belief therein, until your certitude is perfected. So whenever you ascend from a stage of differentiation to a stage of integration, your realization-of-Oneness and your faith will increase, as he says: **And whenever you make your exit from it,**[2] that is, from your sensory perception to your realization-of-Oneness, **your faith,** that is, your belief **will increase,** that is, at the stage of illumination and direct vision, since to exit from one of the two opposites is to enter into the other.

And whenever you emerge, you from you, **your certitude** of Uniqueness **will increase**[3] since the matter will be more complete in you than it is in others. This is the grade of the champions-of-truth *[aṣ-ṣiddīqūn]*, while the first is the grade of the élite of the believers. Certitude is knowledge after doubt, and the term is therefore not applied to perennial knowledge, nor to forms of knowledge that are 'imperative.' What is meant by it here is what he mentions later on, or perhaps what is meant by it is knowledge in an absolute sense, in which case there is no question of contradiction. You should also know that your emerging from you is integration, and the growth of your certitude is the goal of integration, where the Lord of Truth takes control of you. This is the meaning of the [Sacred] Tradition: "I become his hearing by which he hears." Anyone who has not attained it has not achieved perfect certitude, but is deluded, stuck with his formal worship and his attention

[2] In another copy of the text: **from them,** that is, from creatures.

[3] In another manuscript: **will grow stronger.**

to stations and revelations, a prisoner to them because of his love for them, as Walī Raslān indicates when he says:

O prisoner of desires and forms of worship, O prisoner of stations and revelations! You are deluded by what you have been plunged into by illusion and fantasy. **You[4] are preoccupied with you,** to the exclusion of Him (Exalted is He). **Where is the preoccupation with Him** (Exalted is He) **to the exclusion of you,** with your being a prisoner to other than Him?

Anyone who loves a thing is a prisoner to it. Many a one is stuck with desire, and this is the state of the people of heedlessness. Many a one is stuck with formal worship, and this is the state of some of the people devoted to cultivating good behavior. Many a one is stuck with spiritual status, and this is the state of some of the people who develop powers of will. Many a one is stuck with illuminative insight, and this is the state of some of the people concerned with progressive development. Many a one is stuck with Allāh, absorbed in Him to the exclusion of all else, and this is the state of the people of providential favors.

And He (Almighty and Glorious is He) **is Present** with us through His knowledge, **Attentive** to us through His decree, **and He is with you** through His knowledge and His power and His providential care, **wherever you may be in this world or the hereafter.** When you have come to know this, you know that He is with you in private and in public, so be with Him through your absorption in realization-of-Oneness *[tawḥīd]*, because **when you are with Him** like this **He screens you** from you, that is, moves you away from the sight of your own self, so that you are kept safe from hidden idolatry. This is a state that is called annihilation in the realization-of-Oneness *[al-fanā' fi't-tawḥīd]*, or the state of integration *[al-jam']*.

And when you are with you, through your lack of absorption, **He subjects you to serving Him,** that is, He makes you a servant devoted to Him, for He demands of you service to Him. This is the state of differentiation *[farq]*, as referred to previously, in which the individual returns to his formal, outer worship.

Perfect **faith *[īmān]* is your separating from Him** (Exalted is He) by not associating Him with anything belonging to your personal

4 In another MS: **and you.**

attributes, **and certitude *[yaqīn]* is your separating from you,** that is, from your own might, your own strength and your own existence, to witness the perfection of His might, His strength and His existence in place of your impotence and weakness. **When your faith has increased** through separation from all other things, **you will be transported from state to state,** that is, from weakness to strength, till you achieve perfect faith, which is certitude. Then, when your certitude has been perfected, the unseen realms will become visible to you, for perfect faith *[al-īmān al-kāmil]* is now attained.

And when your certitude has increased[5] through your separation from you and from all other things, **you will be transported from station to station,** that is, from gnosis *[maʿrifa]* to illumination *[kashf]*, from illumination to witnessing *[mushāhada]*, from witnessing to direct perception *[muʿāyana]*, from direct perception to contact *[ittiṣāl]*, from contact to annihilation *[fanāʾ]*, from annihilation to perpetuity *[baqāʾ]*, then to other stations familiar to their adepts. You should know that the latter have a Sacred Law *[Sharīʿa]*, namely that you must worship Him (Exalted is He); a 'Procedure' *[Ṭarīqa]*, namely that you must aspire to Him through knowledge and action; and a 'Reality' *[Ḥaqīqa]*, namely that you bear witness to a light which He has deposited in the innermost recess of the heart. You should also know that everything inner has a corresponding outer aspect, and vice-versa.

The Sacred Law is the outer aspect of the Reality, while the Reality is the inner aspect of the Sacred Law, and the pair of them are inseparable as a concept. For a Sacred Law without an inner Reality is useless, and an inner Reality without a Sacred Law is futile.

The three together have been compared to the walnut: The *Sharīʿa* is like the outer shell, the *Ṭarīqa* is like the hidden kernel, and the *Ḥaqīqa* is like the oil within the kernel. There is no way to get at the kernel except by piercing the shell, nor to obtain the oil except by crushing the kernel.

There are several classes of people: Weaklings, they being the common herd; an élite, namely the saints *[al-awliyāʾ]*; and the élite of the élite, namely the Prophets *[al-anbiyāʾ]*. He alludes to this classification when he says:

The Sacred Law *[Sharīʿa]* is for you, O weakling, **until you seek**

[5] In one MS: **has grown strong.**

Him (Exalted is He) **from Him for you,** provided you seek Him with sincerity and honesty, otherwise it is against you, not for you.

And the Reality [*Ḥaqīqa*] is for Him (Exalted is He) **until you seek Him** (Exalted is He) **through Him for Him** (Almighty and Glorious is He), not through you for Him, nor through Him for you, **beyond time**[6] **and beyond space,** by contrast with the *Sharīʿa*, **for the *Sharīʿa*,** because it is a commandment to perform legally prescribed actions, **does have limits [*ḥudūd*],** for example that a particular ritual prayer *[ṣalāt]* shall consist of two cycles or of three, **and modes,** as when the prayer is obligatory or supererogatory, scheduled for a set time or unscheduled. **But the *Ḥaqīqa* has neither limit nor mode,** because it is a spiritual secret, and because one who lives by it is is one who has direct experience of Allāh (Exalted is He), who has shunned creature comforts, for he is at the station of integration, and so always seeks Allāh through Allāh for Allāh. The object of his quest is unlimited, for it is the adored Truth, whereas the object of one who lives by the *Sharīʿa* is limited.

One who lives by[7] **the *Sharīʿa* only**, that is, without the *Ḥaqīqa*, **is given the privilege of striving [*mujāhada*],** namely the practice of external forms of worship and internal servitude. The formal worship is to be practiced by the self *[nafs]*, because it is external, while servitude is for the heart *[qalb]*, because it is internal.

And one who lives by[8] **the *Ḥaqīqa* is given the privilege of grace,** that is, blessing, or, as some say, momentous favor, by which is meant the luminous intimate knowledge which Allāh taught the spirits *[arwāḥ]* when He addressed them with His words: "Am I not your Lord?" (7:172). It is also hinted at by His words: "And He taught Adam all the names." (2:31). But it is buried deep within the spirits, concealed by the gloom of existence and the preoccupations of nature, and only when these vanish away, through the gracious assistance of Allāh, does it become manifest. This is the import of the tradition *[khabar]*: "When someone puts what he knows into practice, Allāh makes him heir to knowledge of what he did not know." Thus that covering is removed from his heart, for he has shunned all that is created, including even Paradise. This person lives by the code of Lordship, while the former lives by the code of formal worship *[ʿibāda]* and servitude *[ʿubūdiyya]*.

[6] In one copy: **beyond limitation.**

[7] In one copy: **with.**

[8] In one copy: **with.**

How great is the contrast between striving and grace, for great is the contrast between one who is assigned to striving without illumination and visionary experience in the situation of differentiation, and one to whom is revealed the secret of Divinity *[al-Ilāhiyya]*, so that he witnesses the meaning of integration through integration *[al-jam' bi'l-jam']*. The stations of differentiation and integration are both to be sought, but to confine oneself to the former is a useless exercise, and to the latter a delusion and a frustration, as has already been indicated in either case.[9]

One who lives with striving, since he is attentive to his actions in keeping with the *Sharī'a*, **is existent** through Allāh, **while one who lives with grace,** since he is living by the code of Lordship, without studying his actions, **is extinct** to all apart from Him (Exalted is He) through his annihilation *[fanā']* in his absorption in Him (Exalted is He).

Practices connected with the perfecting of the servant's outer being, such as the two-fold testimony [professing belief in Allāh as the One Almighty God, and in Muḥammad as His Messenger], observance of the ritual prayer *[ṣalāt]*, payment of the alms-due *[zakāt]*, fasting, pilgrimage *[ḥajj]*, and the holy war *[jihād]*, **are linked to the noble Law *[Shar']*,** by which they have been prescribed.

As for total trust in the Lord *[tawakkul]* and similar virtues connected with the perfection of the inner being, such as abstinence, piety, patience, fear and hope, **this is linked to faith *[īmān]*,** to the belief that Allāh (Exalted is He) "is Doer of what He will." (11:107). Total trust means relying completely on Allāh (Exalted is He), and devoting no attention to material means and the management of them. Some say it means ceasing to exert oneself in areas that are beyond human control, and still other definitions have been given, as I have explained with useful lessons in a commentary on the *Risāla* of al-Qushairī.

And *tawḥīd*, which is your conviction and knowledge of the Oneness of Allāh (Exalted is He), **is linked to the removal,** that is, the removal by Allāh from the servant's vision, **of the veil,** meaning the screens

[9] The commentator now devotes eight lines to a discussion of the Arabic idiom meaning: "How great is the contrast between..." or "What a great difference between..." In one manuscript of the *Risāla*, the particle *mā* is missing between *shattāna* and *baina*, he tells us at the beginning of the above paragraph—where the comment is untranslatable! I omit the linguistic discussion, which would be intelligible—even in translation—only to Arab grammarians.

represented by worldly things, in that he becomes extinct to them and sees them merged into the lights of Divine Majesty. Unveiling is of three kinds: Unveiling of self, unveiling of heart, and unveiling of innermost being, which is the one intended here. The first is designated by the knowledge of certainty *[ʿilm al-yaqīn]*, the second by the essence of certainty *[ʿain al-yaqīn]*, and the third by the truth of certainty *[ḥaqq al-yaqīn]*. All three are sciences *[ʿulūm]*, since they are subdivisions of knowledge *[ʿilm]*, each having its respective subject-matter *[maʿlūm]*: It may be connected with the outer being, in which case it is knowledge of certainty; or with the inner being, in which case it is essence of certainty; or with the Lord of Truth (Exalted is He), in which case it is truth of certainty. You should know that together with unveiling *[kashf]* come the experiences called "being present face-to-face" *[muḥāḍara]*, "disclosure" *[mukāshafa]*, "seeing with one's own eyes" *[muʿāyana]*, and "witnessing" *[mushāhada]*, all of which are linked to *tawḥīd*, and these I have explained in the commentary referred to above.

And people wander astray, deviate, **from the Lord of Truth** (Exalted is He) through seeking Him **with the** natural, corporeal **mind** *[al-ʿaql aṭ-ṭabīʿī al-juthmānī]*, because it is screened by its isolation from the Divine Epiphanies *[at-tajalliyāt al-Ilāhiyya]* and Sublime Gnoses *[al-maʿārif al-Rabbāniyya]*, being confined to such beauty or ugliness, error or correctness, as is contained in external forms *[ṣuwar]*. In contrast to this is the luminous, spiritual mind *[al-ʿaql al-rūḥānī an-nūrānī]*, which is angelic, and with which there is no wandering astray. **And** they wander astray **from the** life they should enjoy in the **hereafter**, by seeking it **with passion**, that is, the passion and appetite of the self *[nafs]*, because it can only be attained through the striving prescribed by the Sacred Law. **So when you seek the Lord of Truth with the** aforementioned **mind, you lose the way** to contact with Him. (**And when you seek the hereafter with passion, you** are sure to **slip.**)

The perfect **believer**, namely one who purifies himself of both obvious and hidden idolatry, **sees by the light of Allāh,** that is, the grace that is generously bestowed upon him, since things are thereby revealed to him in constant succession. "Is he who was dead, and We have raised him to life...?" (6:122). "Beware of the perspicacity of the believer, for he sees by the light of Allāh!" **And one who knows by direct**

experience ***[al-ʿārif]***, namely one who is absorbed in Allāh to the exclusion of all besides Him, **beholds Him by it,** that is, by the light of Allāh, through the lifting of the veil of heedlessness from his heart.

As long as you are with you, that is, with your own self, not absorbed in Us, **We command you,** that is, We oblige you to struggle, because you are at the stage of differentiation. **Then, once you have been rendered extinct,** through your absorption in Us, **to you**, that is, to your own self, **We take charge of you** with attentiveness, providential care and favor, and other benefits that cannot be attained by making efforts, because you are now in integration. **For He does not take charge of them**, that is, the spiritual wayfarers, **until after their annihilation in Him.**

As long as you continue, that is, to see yourself as having existence, action and will, **you are a seeker** ***[murīd]*****. Then, when He,** your Lord, **has made you extinct to you, you are one who is sought** ***[murād],*** so the aim is to make the Lord of Truth the sole object of one's quest, and to shun all that is apart from Him. The seeker is the novice wayfarer, who still sees himself as having existence and action, while the sought is he who is looked upon with the eye of Divine Providence, he who is absorbed in Allāh (Exalted is He). Thus the seeker must shoulder the burden of toil, while the sought has the burden lifted off him—and what a great difference there is between the burdened bearer and the one who is carried and supported!

The most lasting[10] **certainty is your absence from you and your presence with Him** (Exalted is He)[11] which means that you become absent from all that is apart from Him (Exalted is He). Certainty has three states: initial, intermediate and final, along the lines of the knowledge, the essence and the truth of certainty. The first of these is unlikely to endure, because traces of outer attachment still remain. The second and third are enduring, but the third is most lasting, since it is a witnessing through the unveiling of the secret, and this is the highest of the degrees of certainty. So be in your certainty with Allāh alone, and take heed!

What a big difference between what is at His command (Exalted is He), in the way of various prescribed forms of worship and efforts of striving, **and what is because of Him** (Exalted is He), in the way of

[10] One MS adds the gloss: **necessary**.

[11] One MS has "**absence.., presence...**" without "**your**".

various Divine favors and gifts of grace! **If you are at His command** (Exalted is He), practicing the formal worship required of you, **worldly means will be subservient to you,** that is, Allāh (Exalted is He) will facilitate such things for you. As Allāh (Exalted is He) has said:

> Whoever is dutiful toward Allāh, He prepares a way out for him, and provides for him from sources he could never imagine. (65:2,3).

He also says (Exalted is He):

> And whoever is dutiful toward Allāh, He makes his course easy for him. (65:4).

And if you are because of Him (Exalted is He), in that you witness nothing other than Him, **the whole universe will be submissive,** that is, will yield and humble itself, **to you,** so that nothing in it will obstruct your vision of its Creator.

Thus a traveler on the spiritual path is either one who knows Allāh, so that he witnesses things through Allāh, or one who knows the rules, and this latter is he who proceeds by investigation and reasoning, so that he witnesses Allāh through things. The former belongs among the champions of truth and the faithful witnesses, and his language is integration, while the latter belongs among the righteous, and his language is differentiation.

Since there are several distinct stations for the spiritual wayfarer, after repentance, he goes on to describe them as follows:

The first of the stations is patience *[ṣabr]*, that is, self-restraint **in obedience to His will** (Exalted is He), or, as some would say, imposing on the self the hardships of religious duty in pursuit of the attendant reward. **The one in the middle is contentment with,** that is, cheerful acceptance of, **His wishes** (Exalted is He), that is, with respect to His will (it may be necessary to be specific about this to rule out contentment with unbelief and other unlawful things). **And the last is that you come to be with His purpose** (Exalted is He), so that you become an one who knows by direct experience *[ʿārif]*. For when the servant is patient, he achieves contentment, and when he achieves contentment he is with the purpose of Allāh (Exalted is He), and so he becomes extinct to his own action, speech and strength, through a visionary experience from the Divine Presence *[al-Ḥaḍra ar-Rabbāniyya]*, because one who becomes extinct to all that, is permanently with Allāh. His hearing, his seeing and the rest are then as in the [Sacred] Tradition: "I become his hearing by which he hears...." The station of annihilation *[fanā']* is the station of the élite, namely the station of servitude. Thus the patient servant is at the station of worshipful service, while the contented servant is at the station of servitude, and each of them sees himself as having existence and action. One who knows by direct experience is at the station of servitude, but does not see himself as having existence and action, because he lives by Allāh for Allāh, not by his own self for his own self, nor by his own self for Allāh.

Practical knowledge is the way of action, since no action can be correct unless there is knowledge of its nature, **and action is the way of** intimate **knowledge.** As Allāh (Exalted is He) has said: "Be dutiful toward Allāh, and Allāh will teach you." (2:282). And the Prophet (Allāh bless him and give him peace) has said: "When someone puts what he knows into practice, Allāh makes him heir to knowledge of what he did not know." **And** intimate **knowledge is the way of experience of Allāh *[al-ma'rifa bi'llāh]*,** because this is only achieved through the familiarity Allāh provides to assist you, for He (Exalted is He) makes Himself familiar to His servants to the extent He has granted them intimate knowledge *[al-'ilm al-ladunī]*. One to whom He has made Himself familiar knows himself and knows his Lord; he who knows his Lord becomes ignorant of his own self. Thus familiarity is linked to conversance with the self, conversance with the self is linked to conversance with the Lord, and conversance with the Lord is linked to ignorance of the self. According to the Tradition: "He among you who is most conversant with his own self, is the one among you who is most conversant with his Lord."

And experience of Allāh is the way of unveiling *[kashf]* the realities of things, **while unveiling is the way of extinction *[fanā']*** to all apart from Allāh (Exalted is He), in that you see nothing other than Him, because when the servant knows that he is a created being, and that every created being is ephemeral, he recognizes through his own perception that he is ephemeral too. Then the extinction of extinction *[fanāʾ al-fanāʾ]* is that you do not notice your own extinction; this is called perpetuity *[baqāʾ]*, which is interpreted as your seeing that Allāh encompasses everything. **Extinction is in respect of action, then essence, then Truth,** because extinction has three subdivisions: Extinction in respect of deeds *[afʿāl]*, according to the saying: "There is no doer *[fāʿil]* except Allāh," ... (gap in the text at this point).... These three are referred to in the saying of one those who know by direct experience: "When someone witnesses creatures as having no doing *[fiʿl]*, he is on the way to success; when he witnesses them as having no life, he has achieved success; and when he witnesses them as essentially non-existent, he has arrived."

You have not been fit, that is, you are unfit, **for Us as long as there is still within you any remnant of anything apart from Us,** be it of this world or of the hereafter, because you are then unfit for the station of servitude, which is the station of "through Allāh for Allāh," because you have committed a heinous sin. For one of the sins they regard as heinous is that you should see yourself as having any existence together with Allāh (Exalted is He). This is indicated by al-Junaid in his saying: "Your existence is a sin beyond comparison with any other sin." **So when**[12] **you have shifted everything else** away from you, by separating from it, even from extinction,[13] **We shall make you extinct,** through Our knowledge and Our light, **to you,** so that you will cease to see yourself as having any existence. Instead, you will see existence through Allāh, as belonging to Allāh, for your heart will have become an abode for Our Divine Secret. The true meaning of this cannot be conceived by the thinking mind, nor can the tongue express it in words. **Now you have become fit for Us, so we have entrusted you with Our secret,** for he was not fit for the secret until his Lord had made him extinct to him, and made him permanent for Him, so that he became a free man, emancipated from slavery to any other, and a repository for secrets. Thus what is required is complete separation from everything apart from Him (Exalted is He).

And when there does not remain [with you any self-motivation, your certitude is perfected, and when there does not remain] any existence of yours with you, in that you have become extinct to all

[12] In one MS, simply "**When**".

[13] One MS reads: **you have been shifted away from everything else.**

apart from Him (Exalted is He), **your realization-of-Oneness *[tawḥīd]* is perfected,** through your inability to grasp the direct knowledge *[maʿrifa]* that you have received, for it is beyond the utmost limit of comprehension, as indicated by the Tradition: "Glory be to You! We do not know the truth as it is known to You." Also by the Tradition: "When someone knows Allāh, his tongue fails."

The people of the inner, that is, of Reality *[Ḥaqīqa]*, **are with certainty,** because of their freedom from the delusion of outer formalities, and because intimate knowledge is revealed to them, so they see it with their own eyes and witness it directly, and thus come to possess a firm, decisive certitude. The beginning of certitude is disclosure, then comes direct vision, then witnessing. This is why ʿAmr ibn ʿAbd Qais said: "Even if the covering were to be removed, I could not be any more certain." **And the people of the outer,** that is, of the *Sharīʿa*, **are with faith** in the unseen, in witnessing, because formalities persist due to their being stuck with the external features of faith. **So when the heart of the master of certainty stirs for anything other than Allāh,** through his paying momentary attention to some state, station or whatever else, **his certainty is deficient**, according to the people of the inner. **And when no notion ever occurs to him,** of anything other than Allāh, **his certainty is perfect.**

The master of certainty must therefore maintain incessant vigilance, watching over the secret by keeping his attention on the Truth in spite of all distractions. His condition may be likened to the condition of a cat while it is in the state of concentration on its prey. If the concentration is disrupted, the target is missed. **And when the heart of the master of faith** in the unseen **is stirred by**[14] **anything other than the Divine command, his faith is defective,** because faith is diminished by disobedience, just as it is increased by obedience, as we may infer from the Tradition: "The sexual offender is no believer at the time when he commits his offense." **And when it is stirred by the Divine command,** and he carries it out, **his faith** in Allāh (Exalted is He) **is complete.**

The sin of the people of certainty is unbelief, according to them, because one must be absolutely sincere about it, and also because the

[14] In one manuscript: **for.**

virtues of the pious are the vices of those brought near [to the Lord]. The higher the climb, the farther the fall. My master ʿUmar ibn al-Fāriḍ spoke of this [in poetry]:

Were it ever to occur to me to wish for anything but You,
For my heedless notion I would judge myself guilty of apostasy!

Such things are hidden from all but the people of certainty. **And the sin of the people of faith is falling short** therein, because of what has already been explained.

You should know that a "notion" *[khāṭir]* is received by the heart through the will of the Lord. There are five types:

1. Lordly notion *[khāṭir Rabbānī]*, which is an inspired idea *[hājis]*; and intimate knowledge *[al-ʿilm al-ladunī]* is never wrong;
2. Angelic notion *[khāṭir malakī]*;
3. Mental *[ʿaqlī]*;
4. Sensual *[nafsānī]*;
5. Satanic *[shaiṭānī]*.

The Lordly *[Rabbānī]* kind is received from the Presence of Lordship *[Ḥaḍrat ar-Rubūbiyya]*, from the Presence of All-Mercifulness *[Ḥaḍrat ar-Raḥmāniyya]*, and from the Presence of Divinity *[Ḥaḍrat al-Ilāhiyya]*. The difference between these is that the Lordly comes with Majesty *[jalāl]*, the All-Merciful with Beauty *[jamāl]*, and the Divine with Perfection *[kamāl]*. The first erases and annihilates, the second establishes and makes permanent, and the third improves and guides. In Majesty the servant is equipped with patience, in Beauty with gratitude, and in Perfection with serenity.

All three belong to those who know by direct experience *[al-ʿārifīn]*. The angelic and intellectual notions belong to the people of striving *[ahl al-mujāhada]*, while the sensual and satanic belong to the people of heedlessness *[ahl al-ghafla]*. When a notion lingers, it becomes a "concern" *[hamm]*. When it is reinforced, it becomes a "resolution" *[ʿazm]*. Just before action is taken, it becomes a "plan" *[qaṣd]*, and when action is initiated, a "definite intention" *[niyya]*.

The dutiful servant *[al-muttaqī]*[15] at the start of his training **is diligent** in performing his worship with honesty and sincerity, so that he will be guided to the path of truth. As Allāh (Exalted is He) has said: "As for those who strive in Our cause, We shall surely guide them to Our paths." (29:69). And as a certain wise man said: "If someone has not been devoted to striving at the outset, he will never get a sniff of this path." **And the** genuine **lover *[al-muḥibb]* is totally trusting,** that is, confident in relying on his Beloved, because when, after striving, he enters the presence of the Beloved and sees Allāh's gracious favor toward him, he becomes extinct to his work and his existence, and puts all his trust in his Lord (Exalted is He). Thus the diligent one is devoted to his work and his existence, while the lover has been rendered extinct to both of these by his absorption in his Beloved, so he is at ease in his contemplation of Him. **And he who knows by direct experience *[ʿārif]*** of Allāh **is serene;** he makes no movement, nor does any notion occur to him, except with His permission. **And he who is found** with Allāh **is lost** to all that is apart from Him (Exalted is He). You must therefore know that **there is no rest for a dutiful servant**, because he is on the move in the diligent performance of his worship; **and no movement for a lover,** because he has become extinct to his own purpose in the purpose of his Beloved; **and no resolve for one who knows by direct experience,** because he sees nothing in existence except Allāh, since he has become extinct to his own existence and his own will in Allāh's will and His existence, so he sees nothing to resolve upon; **and no being found for the lost,** that is, for one who has vanished from his own sight into the One he has found.

You should also know that the first of the stations is repentance, and the last of them is direct experience *[maʿrifa]*, which follows on from love *[al-maḥabba]*. Love comes after certainty, as he says: **Love arises only after certainty** of the Beloved's existence, for how could one love something before becoming aware of it? **And when the lover is sincere in his love, his heart must be empty of all that is apart from Him** (Exalted is He), because the reality of love is witnessing the Beloved, and this is achieved only after annihilation of the self and the purification of the heart from all that is apart from Him (Exalted is He). **And as long**

[15] One copy has [the synonymous] ***at-taqī.***

as it retains any trace of love for anything but Him, even for love, **he is lacking in love** where Allāh is concerned.

He who takes delight in misfortune, and endures it with patience because of the rewards he sees in it, **co-exists therewith, and he who takes delight and rejoices in prosperity co-exists with it, so when Allāh** (Exalted is He) **makes him extinct,** that is, makes the one who takes delight in each case extinct to his respective enjoyment,[16] **the enjoyment of misfortune and prosperity**[17] **departs**, because the bewilderment experienced in witnessing the Beloved is so overwhelming.

The lover's breath, metonymy for his speech, **is wisdom**, because he witnesses nothing but his Beloved and hears only from Him, so that he utters nothing but wisdom, since this is the understanding of Allāh. **As for the loved one,** because he is drawn ever closer to his Lord through His great love for him, **his breath is power,** moving in the universe through the help of the Munificent King. For the lover is a spiritual traveler who becomes ecstatic, that is, of his own volition, while the loved one is an ecstatic who travels the path. The latter is higher and more special than the lover, because he is sought while the lover is a seeker.

Other types, mentioned in the exhaustive treatises, are the unsuccessful ecstatic *[majdhūb abtar]* and the unsuccessful traveler *[sālik abtar]*. Then there is the ascetic devotee, the type who pays attention to his own existence and seeks the recompense for his efforts, as the author points out when he goes on to say: **Formal acts of worship are for the compensations.** As Allāh (Exalted is He) has said: "Anyone who brings a good deed will receive tenfold the like thereof." (6:160).

And love is for the nearnesses, that is, for the sake of getting close to Him (Exalted is He) through honesty and sincerity.

You should also know that the believers fall, not of their own volition, into five classes: The first two, although there are differences between them, comprise the ordinary believers. The third comprises the élite among them; the fourth, the élite of their élite, namely the lovers; and

[16] Treating the pronoun [Arabic "*-hu*", meaning "him"] as referring back to the [Arabic] word "*man*" [translated above as "he who"]. In another manuscript, however, the text reads: **"So when He makes them extinct to them,"** with both pronouns [Arabic "*-hum*", meaning "them"] in the plural, in keeping with the sense of "*man*" [which could be translated as "those who"], that is, "so when He makes those who take such delight extinct to themselves."

[17] In another copy: **"and of prosperity."**

the fifth, the most special of the special, namely the one who has direct experience of Allāh (Exalted is He) through Allāh, in Allāh, for Allāh *[bi-'llāhi, fi-'llāhi, li-llāhi]*. This is why Allāh (Exalted is He) has said in a Sacred Tradition *[ḥadīth qudsī]*: **"I have prepared for My righteous servants"**, namely those with direct experience of Allāh (Exalted is He) *[al-ʿārifūn bi-'llāhi taʿālā]*, **"that which no eye has ever seen, of which no ear has ever heard, and of which has never occurred to a human heart."**

Such are the servants of the Benefactor, not the servants of the benefaction, and few indeed are they. As Allāh (Exalted is He) has said: "Except those who believe and do good works," (103:3) and how few are they! Physically they are with creatures, but in their hearts they are with the Lord of Truth, never relaxing their contemplation of Him for the twinkling of an eye. He also said in a Sacred Tradition, cited by the author: **"When they,"** that is, those who know Me by experience, **"wish for Me, I give them that which no eye has ever seen and of which no ear has ever heard"**, and this, together with what was mentioned before, is the result of the love with which He has provided them.

When He has made you extinct to your passion by decree *[ḥukm]* (reading the middle consonant as *kāf*),[18] that is, by the command sent down from the Presence of Lordship *[Ḥaḍrat ar-Rubūbiyya]* to the tangible world of servitude *[ʿālam ḥissī al-ʿubūdiyya]*, **and to your will through** intimate **knowledge, you will become a servant with undivided loyalty,** that is, devoted solely to Him and free from all apart from Him, **with neither passion nor will of your own,** since you have become extinct to your own self in the manner described, so you know that will belongs only to Allāh (Exalted is He), "and you will not, unless Allāh wills." (76:30 / 81:29). **Then the veil will be lifted for you** from the secrets of Divinity, **so that servitude will vanish away** from you, that is, will depart, **into Oneness, for the servant will be annihilated** therein, **and the Lord (Almighty and Glorious is He) will remain,** so the servant will witness Him through Him.

The whole of the *Shariʿa* is constriction *[qabḍ]*, because it carries the heavy burdens of formal religious worship, and the bearer of burdens is cramped and fatigued. **And the whole of** intimate **knowledge is**

[18] ***Author's note:*** One manuscript has: *ḥilm* [forbearance], with *lām* as the middle consonant; this means tolerating injury and forsaking it, inasmuch as you see whatever flows from anything in the universe as being in Allāh, (Exalted is He).

expansion *[basṭ]*, because it is unveiling and witnessing; for the master of it, work has become a habit in which there is no heaviness or stiff formality. Far from seeing his own existence in his work, he sees that work as a favor and a mercy from Allāh, so he experiences it expansively. **And the whole of direct experience *[maʿrifa]*** of Allāh **is playful teasing,** whereby the servant dallies with his Lord as a husband dallies with his wife, as when she gives him a coquettish display of defiance, although she is not really opposing him at all. This is sheer generosity and gracious favor from Him (Exalted is He), not an incitement intended to provoke. The station of playful teasing is the place for happy relaxation in speech and behavior.

Our method *[ṭarīqa]*, that is, that of the professors of Oneness *[al-muwaḥḥidūn]*, **is love, not** the **labor** of a weary supervised worker, **and annihilation, not perpetuity;** in short, their path is love and annihilation, not labor and perpetuity. Because **when you enter into work,** which means formal worship, **you belong to you, and when you enter into love** for Allāh, and devote yourself sincerely to Him alone, **you belong to Him** (Exalted is He), **since the worshipper lives for his worship,** because he is striving for this and for his own sake, **while the lover lives for his love,** because he is submissive to the grandeur of his Beloved, renouncing all that is apart from Him. One who knows by direct experience *[ʿārif]* is above them both, because he has achieved what neither of them has achieved, and has exceeded them in intimate learning *[ʿulūm laduniyya]*, Divine gnoses *[maʿārif Ilāhiyya]* and spiritual receivings *[wāridāt rūḥāniyya]*.

When you have come to know Him (Exalted is He), inasmuch as you have become aware that He sees you and that He is the Doer, and you have not been concentrating your attention on your work and seeking compensation for it, **your breathing will be through Him** (Exalted is He), **and your movements will belong to Him,** because you will be molded upon His pattern; **but if you are ignorant of Him** (Exalted is He), inasmuch as you have not come to be like this, **your movements will be your own,** because you will witness them arising from you, in contrast to one who knows by direct experience, for he witnesses no doer except Allāh. As Allāh (Exalted is He) has said: "Allāh is the Creator of everything," (39:62) "and Allāh has created you and your actions." (37:96).

The worshipper *[ʿābid]* has no rest, but rather movement, because he is striving, as already described, **and the ascetic *[zāhid]* has no appetite** for anything other than Allāh, **and the champion of Truth *[ṣiddīq]* has no confidence** in any other than Allāh, since honesty is the mainstay of the matter, and the means to its completion, **and he who is endowed with direct experience *[ʿārif]* has neither might nor strength, neither choice nor will, neither movement nor rest,** for he is with Allāh, **and he who is present *[mawjūd]*** with Allāh **has no presence** with his own self, because of his annihilation through his absorption in Allāh, as has previously been explained.

When you have come to be on familiar terms with Him (Exalted is He), in that you have witnessed Him encompassing everything in creation and knowledge, and you have purified yourself of hidden idolatry *[ash-shirk al-khafī]*, **you will be estranged** from everything other than Him, even **from you,** because you used to regard all that as part of you. **If anyone is preoccupied with Us,** and with Our worship, **for his own sake, We shall make him blind** to the vision of inner knowledge, because he is stuck with his work, **but if anyone is preoccupied with Us for Our sake, We shall give him sight** by which to see it, through removing from him the veils of the universe.

When your worldly **passion has faded away, there will be unveiled for you,** O spiritual traveler, **the door of the Lordly Reality *[al-Ḥaqīqa ar-Rabbāniyya]***, inasmuch as it will overwhelm the heart, **so that your own will is annihilated and Oneness is unveiled to you,** for you will see all existence as belonging to Allāh, by a light which Allāh will cast into your heart, **and then you will realize**, because of your extinction to everything other than Him (Exalted is He), **that it is He** (Exalted is He) acting and existing **in us,**[19] for you will see nothing but Him through His providential care.

If you surrender your affairs **to Him,** and give up your self-management to rely on Him entirely, **He will draw you close** by looking upon you with the eye of mercy and providential care. As the Lord's Friend [Abraham] (peace be upon him) said, when Gabriel (peace be upon him) asked him, when they catapulted him with the ballista and sought to make him fall into the fire: "Is there anything you need?"— "As for needing you, oh no! But as for needing Allāh, oh yes indeed!" Then

[19] In one copy: **not you.**

Gabriel said: "Ask Him!" So he said: "His knowledge of my condition is enough for me without my asking!" **But if you argue with Him,** expressing your unwillingness to accept His judgment by saying: "I shall do it this way, so that it will turn out thus, but if I were not to do it this way, it would not be so," **He will send you away,** that is, He will exclude you from His intimate presence.

If you draw near to Him **through Him,** inasmuch as you do not see yourself as having any existence or action beside His existence and His action, **He will bring you close** to Him through beneficence and gracious favor, **but if you draw near** to Him **through you,** in that you see this as possible for you, **He will send you away,** that is, He will shut you out and have nothing to do with you.

If you seek Him for your own sake, in that you seek degrees and charismatic powers from Him, **He will burden you** with work and make you weary, because if someone expects the reward, he is expected to do the work. **But if you seek Him for His sake** (Exalted is He), **He will pamper you,** that is, He will make you one of the people of dalliance, through His sheer generosity and gracious favor, as we have explained previously.

Your nearness to Him (Exalted is He) **is your separation,** through your annihilation, **from you, while your distance** from Him **is your sticking with you,** because you are an obstacle. In His sight, as mentioned earlier, the virtues of the pious are the vices of those brought near. This is relevant to his words: **If you come without you, He will accept you,** and befriend you with His gentle kindness, **but if you come with you,** in that you see yourself as having existence and action, **He will exclude you** from His intimate presence.

The worker, and one who works at his formal worship is no exception, **is hardly likely to be free of attachment to his labor,** because he expects the reward for it, **so be one of the sort who are disposed toward grace,** that is, the grace of Allāh and His kindness to you, **not one of the sort disposed toward work,** so that you may escape attachment to it and bear witness that there is no doer and none existing except Allāh *[lā fāʿila wa-lā mawjūda illa'llāh]*. Thus you may become one of those who know by direct experience *[min al-ʿārifīn]*, because **if you know Him,**

and that He is the only existing doer, **you will come to rest** on Him, when you are in motion and when you are in repose, so that if you speak, you will speak through Him, and if you hear, you will hear from Him, and thus you will have no tongue of your own and no ear. Hence the saying: "The mark of one who knows by direct experience is that he becomes detached from this world and the hereafter." **But if you are ignorant of Him, you will be agitated**, by your concentration on your work and by your pursuit of the reward for it.

So the point of all this **is that He** (Exalted is He) **should be** with you, **and you should not be,** but should rather become extinct to all that is other than He (Exalted is He).

As for the common folk, namely those servants who rank below the enlightened commoners *[ʿawāmm al-ʿārifīn]*, **their works are suspect,** because they expect to receive the reward for them, so they are tainted by their worldly interests, and they are like hirelings: if they are paid their wages, they work, but otherwise not. **And as for the élite,** namely those who transcend their worldly interests, **their works are good deeds, *[qurubāt]***; their attention is directed not toward work or reward, but rather toward nearness *[qurb]* to Him (Exalted is He). **And as for the élite of the élite,** namely those who become annihilated in Allāh, through Allāh, for Allāh, and who continue from Allāh to Allāh, **their works are degrees** in which they ascend, for they do not view themselves as having either work or nearness, but Allāh makes them extinct to them[selves] and perpetuates them for His sake to discharge what is due to Him.

Whenever you shun, O spiritual traveler, **your passion** and your worldly interest, **your faith is reinforced,** for unveiled to you then is the secret of Lordly Wisdom *[al-Ḥikma ar-Rabbāniyya]* and the Divine Power *[al-Qudra al-Ilāhiyya]*, and that He is the only existing doer. **And whenever you shun your own essence *[dhāt]***, that is, become extinct to it, and to all other creatures, and become cast in the mold of the station of perpetuity, inasmuch as you see Allāh encompassing everything, **your realization-of-Oneness is reinforced.** As I have already explained concerning the realization-of-Oneness, there is *tawḥīd* in actions *[fi'l-afʿāl]*, *tawḥīd* in attributes *[fi'ṣ-ṣifāt]*, and *tawḥīd* in essence *[fi'dh-dhāt]*. The first of these is the *tawḥīd* of the commoners *[al-ʿawāmm]*, the second is the *tawḥīd* of the élite *[al-khawāṣṣ]*, and the third is the *tawḥīd* of the élite of the élite *[khawāṣṣ al-khawāṣṣ]*.

Creatures, due to your involvement with them, **are a screen** preventing you from beholding Him (Exalted is He), **and you,** for the same reason, **are a screen** that also gets in the way of it. **But the Lord of Truth *[al-Ḥaqq]* is not secluded** from you, since there is no power capable of secluding Him. **It is He Who conceals Himself** from you, since there is no power capable of concealing Him. **And He conceals Himself from you through you,** because of the attention you pay to your own existence and your work. **And you are secluded from you by Him** (Exalted is He),[20] because when you pay attention to His existence (Exalted is He), you are secluded by it from you. **So separate from you,** that is, from your existence and your power and your strength, **and you shall witness** all the blessings and generous favor He has graciously bestowed upon you.

Peace be upon you and the mercy of Allāh and His blessings!

[20] Instead of **by Him,** one manuscript has **by them,** that is, by creatures.

Sharḥ Fatḥ ar-Raḥmān

Commentary on the *Risāla* of Walī Raslān[1]

by

'Alī ibn 'Aṭiyya 'Alawān al-Ḥamawī

(d. A.H. 936/1530 C.E.)

[1] In this translation of *Sharḥ Fatḥ ar-Raḥmān*, words that occur in the text of the *Risāla* of Walī Raslān are printed in bold font. A romanized transliteration, in italicized bold font, has been supplied in the footnotes.

In the Name of Allāh the All-Merciful and Compassionate.[2]

Praise be to Allāh,[3] the Lord of All the Worlds. Blessing and peace be upon our Master Muḥammad, and upon his family and his Companions, each and every one.

Now then,[4] the most meritorious of all good works *[qurubāt]*, and the most excellent of all forms of worshipful obedience *[ṭā'āt]*, are self-abasement *[dhilla]*, contrite humility *[inkisār]*, and casting oneself down *[inṭirāḥ]* at the gate of the Lord *[Mawlā]* in the utmost state of destitution. You must therefore cast yourself down, O tenderhearted brother, at the gate of your Lord. You must purify your clothes by ridding them of the filthy stain of polytheism *[shirk]*, so that you may experience the real meaning of your ritual prayer *[ṣalāt]* and attain to your true nobility.

You must also **know that,**[5] if you adopt an attitude of strict impartiality *[inṣāf]* and view your situation with a discerning eye, and if the gifts of grace *[alṭāf]* assist you in the process, you will come to understand what [Walī Raslān] means when he says, speaking as one who knows from direct experience *['ārif]*: **"The whole of you is covert polytheism."**[6]

[2] ***Bismi 'llāhi 'r-raḥmāni 'r-raḥīm.***

[3] ***al-ḥamdu li-'llāh.*** (In this manuscript of *Sharḥ Fatḥ ar-Raḥmān*, these words have been written in a different shade of ink from that used for the text of the commentary, apparently indicating that they occur in the *Risāla* of Walī Raslān. In Zakariyyā' al-Anṣārī's *Kitāb Fatḥ ar-Raḥmān*, however, these words are not quoted as part of the *Risāla*.)

[4] ***ammā ba'du.*** (In Zakariyyā' al-Anṣārī's *Kitāb Fatḥ ar-Raḥmān*, the alternative form *wa ba'du* is quoted from the text of the *Risāla*.)

[5] ***wa ' 'lam anna.***

[6] ***kullaka shirkun khafiyyun.*** (In works devoted to this subject, the expression *shirk laṭīf* [subtle polytheism] is often used as an alternative to *shirk khafī* [covert/hidden/concealed polytheism]. (See: G.W.J. Drewes, *Directions for Travellers on the Mystic Path*. The Hague, Netherlands: Martinus Nijhoff, 1977, pp. 22 and 23.)

What he is saying, in effect, is that every aspect and facet of your being, your dealings and your attitudes, your appetites and your manifest behavior, all amount to a form of polytheism *[shirk]* that is blatantly overt *[ẓāhir]* from the perspective of those with developed faculties of insight *[arbāb al-baṣīrāt]*, although it is covert *[khafī]* from the standpoint of someone who has not reached that stage of development, and whose conscience *[sarīra]* is not yet clear.

When someone attaches little importance *[takhaffafa]* to worshipful servitude *[ʿubūdiyya]*, he takes a pretentious view of his own deeds and a distorted view of his own words, and it is only to someone who is seriously committed *[taḥaqqaqa]* to worshipful servitude that the significance of this concept can be fully apparent. As an example of such dedicated commitment, let us consider the case of our Master [the Caliph] ʿUmar [ibn al-Khaṭṭāb] (may Allāh be well pleased with him), and how he once surprised Ḥudhaifa[7] (may Allāh be well pleased with him) by asking him the question: "Am I one of the hypocrites *[munāfiqīn]*?" "No," replied Ḥudhaifa, "you are not one of them, and no one after you will ever be as innocent of hypocrisy as you are!" If a man like ʿUmar (may Allāh be well pleased with him) could harbor such a grave suspicion about his own lower self *[nafs]*, and could subject it to this kind of scrutiny, what does this tell us about everyone else?

That [kind of dedicated commitment] develops out of the lack of satisfaction with the lower self *[ʿadam ar-riḍā ʿani 'n-nafs]* that is the very root of all forms of worshipful obedience *[aṣl aṭ-ṭāʿāt]*. The root of every act of worshipful obedience, of every moment of vigilant awareness *[yaqẓa]*, and of every virtue *[ʿiffa]*, is the lack of satisfaction with the lower self, just as positive satisfaction with it is the root of every sinful act of disobedience *[maʿṣiya]*, every moment of heedless negligence *[ghafla]*, and every lustful indulgence *[shahwa]*.

[7] Abū ʿAbdi'llāh Ḥudhaifa ibn [the son of] al-Yamān al-ʿAbasī (may Allāh be well pleased with them both) was among the earliest to embrace Islām, and he came to be one of the most distinguished of all the Companions of the Prophet (Allāh bless him and give him peace). He was famous for his dedication to an abstinent way of life. Together with Abū 'd-Dardāʾ and Abū Dharr (may Allāh be well pleased with them both), he was one of those Companions who were called *ṣāḥib sirr an-Nabī*, because of the secret knowledge imparted to them by the Prophet (Allāh bless him and give him peace). He died in A.H. 36.

Shaikh Abu 'l-Ḥasan ash-Shādhilī[8] (may Allāh be well pleased with him) was making a very similar point when he said: "If someone dies without having penetrated deeply into this science *['ilm]* of ours, he may die while still persisting in the commission of major sins *[kabā'ir]*."

He was stating the simple truth when he uttered these words, and he was stating it without exaggeration. As a matter of fact, he was elucidating and clarifying one of the sayings of the Chief of the Masters of Perfection *[Sayyid Arbāb al-Kamāl]* (Allāh bless him and give him peace), namely:

> There are three things that lead to salvation *[munjiyāt]*, and there are three things that lead to perdition *[muhlikāt]*. As for the things that lead to salvation, they are: (1) dutiful devotion *[taqwā]* to Allāh both in private and in public, (2) speaking the truth *[qawl al-ḥaqq]* whether one is in a state of contentment or a state of exasperation, and (3) frugality *[qaṣd]* in affluence and poverty alike. As for the things that lead to perdition, they are: (1) a whimsical passion pursued *[hawā muttaba']*, (2) a mean-spirited impulse obeyed *[shuḥḥ muṭā']*, and (3) a man's conceited satisfaction with his own lower self *[i'jāb bi-nafsih]*, this being by far the most serious of them all.

Pay close attention to his words (Allāh bless him and give him peace): "... this being by far the most serious of them all"! Having stated that the causes of perdition *[muhlikāt]* are three in number, namely, ostentation *[riyā']*, envy *[ḥasad]* and vanity *['ujb]*, he declares that vanity is by far the most serious of the three. So tell me, O my brother, do we know of any person who performs the ritual prayer *[ṣalāt]* without taking

[8] Shaikh Abu 'l-Ḥasan 'Alī ibn 'Abd'illāh ash-Shādhilī (may Allāh be well pleased with him) was born in the Tunisian village of Ghumāra in A.H. 593/1196 C.E. After receiving instruction from Abū 'Abd'illāh Muḥammad ibn Ḥarāzim, he became a pupil of the famous Abū Madyan (may Allāh bestow His mercy upon them). He traveled to the East in A.H. 615, but returned to the West some years later, on the advice of Shaikh Abu 'l-Fatḥ al-Wāsiṭī (may Allāh bestow His mercy upon him). Persecution eventually forced him to take refuge in Egypt, where he won great renown, among the scholars *['ulamā']* as well as the common people. He made a practice of performing the Pilgrimage *[Ḥajj]* every year, and died at Ḥumaithrā on the Red Sea coast while returning from Mecca in A.H. 656/1258 C.E.

In his discourses, Shaikh Abu 'l-Ḥasan ash-Shādhilī (may Allāh be well pleased with him) is said to have emphasized five basic principles, namely: (1) devotion to Allāh in private and in public life; (2) adherence to the Sunna of the Prophet (Allāh bless him and give him peace) in word and deed; (3) detachment from one's fellow creatures in prosperity and in adversity alike; (4) patient acceptance of the Will of Allāh (Exalted is He) in all things great and small; (5) turning toward Allāh (Almighty and Glorious is He) in joy and sorrow alike.

conceited pride in his performance of that prayer? Do we know of any person who keeps the fast *[ṣawm]* without taking conceited pride in his observance of the fast?

Of course we know of no such person, unless it be someone whom Allāh has enabled to succeed *[waffaqa]* by virtue of His providential care *[ʿināya]*, and whom He has enfolded in the blessed grace *[baraka]* of His saints *[awliyāʾ]* and His special friends *[khāṣṣa]*, for they are the physicians who are qualified to treat the diseases of our hearts. They can fairly be described as the tried and tested antidote *[tiryāq]* to the poisons that are sins. I urge you therefore, O my brother, to spend time in their company, in order that you may reap the blessed benefits of associating with them and gather their ripe fruit. As a result of this, your habitual pattern of faults and failings will become apparent to you, and, through the blessed grace of their instruction, you will be cleansed of every form of polytheism *[shirk]* that screens you from the One who knows all mysteries through and through *[ʿAllām al-Ghuyūb]*.

Once you have progressed to this level of purification, you will come to be detached from your ordinary human characteristics *[awṣāf bashariyya]*. You will come to be far removed from any characteristic that is incompatible with worshipful servitude *[ʿubūdiyya]*. The realization-and-affirmation-of-Oneness *[tawḥīd]* will come to be evident and plainly manifest. Your lower self *[nafs]* will fade into nonexistence and you will make your exit from it. And that is the greatest bliss *[an-naʿīm al-akbar]*!

As he [Walī Raslān] (may Allāh be well pleased with him) has said: **"And your realization-and-affirmation-of-Oneness will not become evident to you until you exit from you[rself]."**[9] In other words, the spiritual station of the affirmation-of-Oneness *[maqām at-tawḥīd]* will not become a reality for you, the pure wine *[sulāfa]* of its true meaning will not be sucked into you, not one of its distinctive features will be glimpsed by you, and nearness to its inner courtyard and sanctuary will not be permitted to you—not until you have made your exit from you, that is, from your own lower self *[nafs]*, through your detachment from your ordinary human characteristics *[awṣāf bashariyya]*, the abandonment of your personal preferences *[ikhtiyārāt]* and considerations

[9] ***wa mā yabīnu la-ka tawḥīduka illā idhā kharajta ʿan-ka.***

[tadabburāt], and confirmation of the fact that you have indeed arrived at the station of worshipful servitude *[maqām al-ʿubūdiyya]*.

Then, and only then, the lights of the affirmation-of-Oneness *[anwār at-tawḥīd]* will shine upon you, and the rays of direct knowledge *[maʿrifa]* and singular devotion *[tafrīd]* will stream forth from your heart. As far as your outwardly visible form *[ẓāhir]* is concerned, you will be in the company of your fellow creatures *[khalq]*, but your inner being *[bāṭin]* will be in the company of the Divine Truth *[Ḥaqq]*. Your outwardly visible form will be dedicated to the practice of the Sacred Law *[Sharīʿa]*, while your inner being will be dedicated to the experience of Reality *[Ḥaqīqa]*.

You will demonstrate the distinction [between truth and falsehood], and not only your tongue but all the members of your body will bear witness thereto. The lights of integration *[jamʿ]* will radiate upon you, so that your innermost being *[sirr]*, your spirit *[rūḥ]* and your heart's core *[janān]* will come to be imbued therewith.

You will eat from the fruit of the tree of "*Lā ilāha illa'llāh* [There is none worthy of worship but Allāh]" with your Lord's permission at any time and on any occasion. You will parade in the splendid clothes of "*Muḥammadar Rasūlu'llāh* [Muḥammad is the Messenger of Allāh]," so every spectator will look upon you with honor and every eye will view you with favor.

You will advance from the station of faith *[īmān]* to the station of active goodness *[iḥsān]*, at which point Reality *[Ḥaqīqa]* will be disclosed to you, and the true state of affairs will become manifestly obvious to your sight. You must therefore seek forgiveness for all the patterns of behavior by which your character has previously been defined. You must also confess your sins, for the gifts of grace *[alṭāf]* encompass one who confesses to having sinned.

As he [Walī Raslān] (may Allāh be well pleased with him) has said: **"Provided you are sincere, it will be disclosed to you that it is He, not you, so you must ask forgiveness for you."**[10] In other words, as soon as the actual fact of the matter *[ḥaqīqat al-amr]* has been disclosed to you, as soon as your perception has been clarified and confirmed by the radiant lights of the affirmation-of-Oneness *[tawḥīd]*, and as soon as

[10] ***fa-kulla-mā akhlaṣta yukshafu la-ka anna-hu Huwa lā anta fa-tastaghfir min-ka.***

your conscience *[sarīra]* is clear, it will be patently obvious to you that it is He, Allāh (Exalted is He), not you, to whom you should ascribe [control of all] affairs, and on whom you are utterly dependent in all your activities and situations, because He is the Independent Agent *[Mutaṣarrif]* in charge of all things, the Managing Director *[Mudabbir]* of all things, the Mover *[Muḥarrik]* of all things and the One who brings movement to a halt *[Musakkin]*. Indeed, not a glance is cast by anyone's eye, and not a thought occurs to anyone's mind, except through His Will *[Irāda]* and His Power *[Qudra]*. As He has told us (Exalted is He):

> And Allāh has created you and whatever you make or do. (37:96)[11]

Once you have come to understand what this means, once the significance of it has taken control of your heart, once you can recognize the reality *[ḥaqīqa]* of what this is about, and once its implications for you personally are as clear to you as its general import, you will no longer entertain the slightest doubt that it is He who is the Doer *[Fa''āl]*, not you. You will therefore seek forgiveness for you, that is to say, for your own lower self *[nafs]*, its states *[aḥwāl]* and its attributes *[ṣifāt]*.

Once you have fully realized, O my brother, that your lower self is made up entirely of sins, and that its characteristics and conditions are nothing but faults and failings, once you have actually arrived at the station of worshipful servitude *['ubūdiyya]* and readiness to seek forgiveness *[istighfār]*, once you have begun to demonstrate a greater capacity for self-abasement *[dhilla]* and humble contrition *[inkisār]*, and once you have adopted compliance with the Sacred Law *[imtithāl ash-Sharī'a]* as your watchword, and conduct in accordance with the manners of the Spiritual Path *[ta'addub bi-ādāb aṭ-Ṭarīq]* as your regular style of dress, then, O my brother, the station of the affirmation-of-Oneness *[maqām at-tawḥīd]* will be made manifest to you, and its peculiar properties *[mashārib]* will become clearly apparent. The gloom of polytheism *[shirk]* will depart from you, and its dark hues will vanish away.

As he [Walī Raslān (may Allāh be well pleased with him)] has said: **"And whenever you encounter [any form of it],[12] your own polytheism will be evident to you. You must therefore renew, in**

[11] *wa 'llāhu khalaqakum wa mā ta'malun.*

[12] The words ***naw'an min-hu*** **[any form of it]** are omitted from the quotation given in this manuscript text of *Sharḥ Fatḥ ar-Raḥmān*, although they do occur in Zakariyyā' al-Anṣārī's *Kitāb Fatḥ ar-Raḥmān*.

every hour and at every moment, an affirmation-of-Oneness and a faith."[13]. In other words, whenever you acknowledge the fact that it is Allāh (Exalted is He) who is the Independent Agent *[Mutaṣarrif]* in charge of all affairs, not anyone apart from Him, when you genuinely experience at that moment the reality of "*Lā ilāha illa 'llāh* [There is none worthy of worship except Allāh]" and intuitively recognize that there is no cause of harm *[lā ḍārr]*, no source of benefit *[lā nāfiʿ]*, no giver *[lā muʿṭī]*, no withholder *[lā māniʿ]*, no keeper *[lā ḥāfiẓ]* and no uplifter *[lā rāfiʿ]* except Allāh, and when this direct knowledge *[maʿrifa]* is not rejected by your flesh and blood,[14] but comes to be a natural disposition *[sajiyya]* of yours and an attribute of your character, that is when your own polytheism *[shirk]* will be evident to you in all your active movements and your states of rest, your choices and your plans, your public discourse and your manifest behavior. At every moment, therefore, you must renew an affirmation-of-Oneness *[tawḥīd]* and a faith *[īmān]*.

You must heed the advice: "Renew your faith by the frequent invocation *[dhikr]* of '*Lā ilāha illa 'llāh* [There is none worthy of worship except Allāh],'" for this is effective as a broom to sweep away the aliens *[aghyār]*,[15] and as a detergent to remove all aliens from the confines of the heart. That is why He has told us:[16]

> The most excellent invocation is: "'There is none worthy of worship except Allāh' is my fortress," for anyone who enters My fortress will be safe from My chastisement.[17]

If a person has entered inside the fortress of his Master *[Mawlā]*, how can he be accessible to anyone apart from Him? The spiritual traveler *[sālik]* must therefore make a constant practice of repeating this invocation with his tongue, until its influence reaches the inner core of his

[13] ***wa kulla-mā wajadta [nawʿan min-hu] bāna la-ka 'sh-shirku fa-tujaddid fī kulli sāʿatin wa waqtin tawḥīdan wa īmānan.***

[14] The expression "your flesh and blood" should be understood in the literal sense of "your physical constitution," not in the figurative sense (common in English but not in Arabic usage) of "the closest members of your family."

[15] The aliens *[aghyār]* are all "others"—all other entities, be they persons, things, or whatever—apart from Allāh (Exalted is He).

[16] Although the author does not say so explicitly, this is clearly a (non-Qurʾānic) Divine Saying *[Ḥadīth Qudsī]*.

[17] *afḍalu 'dh-dhikri "'Lā ilāha illa 'llāhu' ḥisnī" fa-man dakhala ḥisnī amina min ʿadhābī.*

heart *[janān]*. It will thus be the means by which he is able to eradicate polytheism, while all his other supports have collapsed in ruins, since the ordinary weak and incompetent individual is powerless to resist the enemy, except by remembering to invoke his Master *[Mawlā]*. It is quite impossible for him to escape from the savage beasts of polytheism *[shirk]*, except by securing the protection of "'*Lā ilāha illa 'llāhu' ḥiṣnī*' ['There is none worthy of worship except Allāh' is my fortress]." As long as the spiritual traveler *[sālik]* persists in repeating this invocation, his faith *[īmān]* will increase and he will be detached from dependence on his fellow creatures. The more he concentrates his attention upon it, and the more often he repeats it, the more his certitude *[yaqīn]* will increase, until he becomes completely detached from his own lower self *[nafs]* and attains to the Divine Truth *[Ḥaqq]*.

As he [Walī Raslān (may Allāh be well pleased with him)] has said: **"And whenever you become detached from them** [that is, from your fellow creatures]**, your faith will increase; and whenever you become detatched from you, your certitude will increase."**[18]

Becoming detached from your fellow creatures means giving up all reliance on them and ceasing to be dependent on them. Whenever the spiritual traveler *[sālik]* detaches his heart from them, he takes his heart back to his Master *[Mawlā]*, and this is the reality of his faith *[īmān]* and its point of culmination.

It may sometimes be the case, however, that the spiritual traveler *[sālik]* has indeed become detached from his fellow creatures, and yet he still has a residual problem to deal with, inasmuch as he continues to attach importance to the lower self *[nafs]* and its machinations, and still gives consideration to its wishes and preferences. Until he becomes detached from his own self, just as he has already become detached from other people, the station of certitude *[maqām al-yaqīn]* will not be fully accessible to him and he will not be able to experience it completely, for his own self also belongs to the realm of creation *[khalq]*, and the servant cannot attain to the Lord of Truth *[Ḥaqq]* as long as he has not been separated from all connection with His creation. As the saying goes: "The Spiritual Path is both separation *[faṣl]* and reunion *[waṣl]*."

[18] ***wa kulla-mā kharajta min-hum zāda īmānu-ka: wa kulla-mā kharajta min-ka zāda yaqīnu-ka.***

Let us also remind outselves of the words of the author [of the *Risāla*, Walī Raslān] (may Allāh be well pleased with him): **"Whenever you become detached from you, your certitude will increase."**

What a splendid contribution was made by Shaikh ʿAbd al-Qādir [al-Jīlānī] (may Allāh be well pleased with him), when he said, on this very same theme:

> "Once you have died in relation to your fellow creatures, you will hear a voice saying: 'May Allāh bestow His mercy upon you, and may He cause you to die in relation to your whims and passions *[hawā]*!'
>
> "Then, once you have died in relation to your whims and passions *[hawā]*, you will hear a voice saying: 'May Allāh bestow His mercy upon you, and may He cause you to die in relation to your self-will *[irāda]* and your cherished aspirations *[munā]*!'
>
> "Then, once you have died in relation to your self-will *[irāda]*, you will hear a voice saying to you: 'May Allāh bestow His mercy upon you, and may He restore you to life!'
>
> "You will then live a life that has no death to follow it. You will enjoy an affluence that has no poverty to follow it. You will enjoy good health that has no sickness to follow it."

Yes indeed! Why should this not happen to the servant, once he has come to be in the presence of his Master *[Mawlā]*? Why should he not actually experience everything mentioned above, once there is nothing left in his heart except Allāh? If someone matches this description, his interest and concern will have transcended all other entities [apart from Allāh]. He will not focus his attention on any Garden of Paradise nor on any Fire of Hell. He will not rely on formal acts of worship *[ʿibādāt]* and spiritual stations *[maqāmat]*, nor will he depend on revelations *[mukāshafāt]* and visible manifestations *[mushāhadāt]*.

As he [Walī Raslān (may Allāh be well pleased with him)] has said: **"O prisoner of desires and formal acts of worship, O prisoner of stations and revelations! You are deluded and you are preoccupied with you. Where is your preoccupation with Him to the exclusion of you? He** (Almighty and Glorious is He) **is Present and Attentive, 'and He is with you wherever you may be,'[19] in this world and the hereafter."**[20]

[19] The words: "**and He is with you wherever you may be** ***[wa Huwa maʿa-kum aina-mā kuntum]***" are spoken by Allāh (Almighty and Glorious is He) in the Qurʾān (57:4).

[20] ***yā asīra 'sh-shahawāti wa 'l-ʿibādāt: yā asīra 'l-maqāmāti wa 'l-mukāshafāt: anta maghrūrun wa anta mashghūlun bi-ka ʿan-hu: aina ishghālu-ka bi-hi ʿan-ka: Huwa Ḥāḍirun wa Nāẓir: "wa Huwa maʿa-kum aina-mā kuntum" fi 'd-dunyā wa 'l-ākhira.***

He [Walī Raslān] (may Allāh be well pleased with him) has undertaken to provide spiritual travelers *[sālikīn]* with a clear explanation of the path that is followed by those who are genuinely concerned with truth and reality *[ṭarīq ahl at-taḥqīq]*. He is attempting to remove from the confines of their heart the filthy rubbish that hinders their progress *[wasākhat at-taʿwīq]*, since anything on which the spiritual traveler relies and depends can only be an obstacle to him. Even if the thing in question is something pertaining to formal acts of worship *[ʿibādāt]*, or to spiritual stations *[maqāmāt]* and revelations *[mukāshafāt]*, it still represents an obstacle, for if the heart is inclined to form an attachment to the thing, the heart comes to be its prisoner and its slave.

As the saying goes: "You do not love something without becoming a slave to it." But He does not like you to be a slave to anyone or anything other than Him. Just as He does not like the work in which others have a share *[ʿamal mushtarak]*, He does not like the heart in which others have a share *[qalb mushtarak]*. That kind of work is unacceptable to Him, and that kind of heart is likewise unacceptable to Him. You must therefore empty your heart of all alien elements *[aghyār]*. It is filled with all sorts of knowledge *[maʿārif]* and secret thoughts *[asrār]* about formal acts of worship, spiritual stations and revelations, and so, when the spiritual traveler becomes preoccupied with these alien elements and forms an attachment to them, he becomes a prisoner to them. He comes to be deluded by them, in fact, and it is precisely for this reason that he [Walī Raslān] (may Allāh be well pleased with him) has said: **"You are deluded, and you are preoccupied with you to the exclusion of Him."** In other words, you are preoccupied with the interests of your own lower self *[nafs]*, to the exclusion of your Lord.

Your self-preoccupation is bound to be an obstacle to your spiritual progress, so you must abandon it, because He created your heart for no other purpose than to serve as a place devoted to the remembrance of Him. When you make room inside it for anything apart from Him, you are overstepping the limit and committing an outrage.

How splendidly the point was made by a certain righteous man, when he said: "I cannot be counted as one of the lovers [of the Lord] if I do not treat the heart as His House and His Station, and if my circumambulation *[ṭawāf]* is not performed by causing the innermost being *[sirr]* to circle around therein, while He represents my cornerstone *[rukn]* at the point when I am ready to make a 'gesture of reconciliation' *[istilām]*."[21]

In short, as far as things are concerned, it is essential for any would-be traveler on the path of the spiritual élite *[ṭarīq al-khawāṣṣ]* to remain separate from them. That is to say, he must adopt a detached and disinterested attitude toward them, controlling them instead of letting them control him, so that, whatever social and business transactions he may need to conduct with his outer being *[ẓāhir]*, his heart will always be in the presence of his Master *[Mawlā]*.

The sense of this is implicitly conveyed by the saying of the Prophet (Allāh bless him and give him peace):

> And my chief consolation [lit., the cooling of my eye] has been granted [to me] in the ritual prayer *[wa juʿilat qurratu ʿainī fi 'ṣ-ṣalāt]*.[22]

[21] This saying is a spiritual allegory based on the rites of Pilgrimage *[Ḥajj]*. The Kaʿba in the Sanctuary at Mecca is known as the House of Allāh *[Baitu 'llāh]*. It is also called His Station *[Maqām]*, because it is there that the pilgrims stand in readiness to perform their prayers and other rites of worship. The ceremony of circumambulation *[ṭawāf]*, in which the pilgrim makes seven circuits around the Kaʿba, three times with a brisk step and four at an ordinary pace, is enjoined in the verse *[āya]* of the Qurʾān in which Allāh (Almighty and Glorious is He) says to Abraham (peace be upon him):

> Do not associate anything with Me, and purify My House for those who circle around it, and those who stand, and those who bow and make prostration *[lā tushrik bī shaiʾan wa ṭahhir Baitiya li'ṭ-ṭāʾifīna wa 'l-qāʾimīna wa 'r-rukkaʿi 's-sujūd]*. (22:26)

The *rukn* is the corner of the Kaʿba in which the Black Stone is embedded. While the term *istilām* (a derivative of the same triconsonantal root—*s-l-m*—as *Islām, salām*, etc.) is the noun corresponding to the verb *istalama* [he became reconciled], it has acquired a specific meaning in the context of the rites of Pilgrimage, namely: "the act of touching the Black Stone of the Kaʿba, either by kissing it with the lips or stroking it with the hand." The translation 'gesture of reconciliation' has therefore been enclosed between inverted commas.

[22] This is actually the final element in one of the most famous sayings of the Prophet (Allāh bless him and give him peace), a very literal translation of which would read:

> Three things belonging to this world of yours have been made lovable to me: perfume, women, and—the cooling of my eye has been granted [to me] in the ritual prayer *[ḥubbiba ilayya min dunyākum thalāth: aṭ-ṭību wa 'n-nisāʾu wa—juʿilat qurratu ʿainī fi 'ṣ-ṣalāt]*.

The grammatical structure of the saying is interrupted when the third element in the list takes the form, not of a another simple noun, but of a separate sentence, beginning with the verb *juʿilat* (which could also be translated: "has been placed" or, "has been made to reside" or, "has been made available").

Notice that he said "in the ritual prayer *[fī 'ṣ-ṣalāt]*," not "because of the ritual prayer *[bi-'ṣ-ṣalāt]*!"[23] You must reflect on this saying *[ḥadīth]* with careful attention, for the path of those who know by direct experience *[ṭarīq al-ʿārifīn]* will then become manifestly apparent to you, and you will develop a mature understanding of its true significance. You must ponder it carefully with your heart, for then you will discover the straight path *[aṣ-ṣirāṭ al-mustaqīm]*. You will also succeed in grasping the real meaning of "*Lā ilāha illa 'llāh* [There is none worthy of worship except Allāh]," since its real meaning *[ḥaqīqa]* is turning away from all else *[al-iʿrāḍ ʿani 's-siwā]* and devoting oneself entirely to the Master *[al-iqbāl ʿala 'l-Mawlā]*. You must therefore make a diligent effort, O my brother, to ensure that this is a genuine experience as far as your heart is concerned. You must really sink your teeth into the task! You must also ponder it with your rational faculty *[lubb]*.

He (Almighty and Glorious is He) is indeed Present *[Ḥāḍir]* at all times, "and He is with you wherever you may be"[24] in this world and the hereafter, under all circumstances, so be sure to heed this excellent piece of advice:

"Give togetherness *[maʿiyya]*[25] its due, and always be on your

[23] The translator's task becomes extremely delicate in a case like this, where a crucial point hinges on a distinction drawn by the author between two Arabic prepositions. In certain contexts, the prepositions *fī* and *bi-* (the hyphen indicates that *bi-* is joined to the following word in the Arabic script) are virtually synonymous, and in many common phrases they are actually interchangeable. For instance, *bi-maʿiyyati fulān and fī maʿiyyati fulān* both mean "in the company of so-and-so." Nevertheless, in considering the author's emphatic distinction between *fī 'ṣ-ṣalāt* and *bi-'ṣ-ṣalāt*, it seems reasonable to arrive at the following conclusions:

(1) As used in this saying of the Prophet (Allāh bless him and give him peace), the preposition *fī* bears its primary signification, namely, "in; within." The expression *fī 'ṣ-ṣalāt* can therefore be translated: "in (or, within) the *ṣalāt* [the Islāmic ritual prayer]."

(2) When stating so emphatically that the Prophet (Allāh bless him and give him peace) did not use the expression *bi-'ṣ-ṣalāt*, the author expected his readers to understand that he intended the preposition *bi-* to designate instrumentality or agency (in which case it would signify "by means of" or "because of"), and/or commodity value (in which case it would signify "in exchange for" or "at the price of").

[24] *wa Huwa maʿa-kum aina-mā kuntum*. (57:4)

[25] The Arabic word *maʿiyya* is an abstract noun derived from the preposition *maʿa* [(together) with], which occurs in the above-quoted verse *[āya]* of the Qurʾān: "and He is with you *[maʿa-kum]* wherever you may be." According to context, its English equivalent may therefore be "togetherness," or "company," or "concomitance," or "simultaneity." In addition to its abstract meanings, however, as the anonymous author of the saying, "Give *maʿiyya* its due ..." was certainly aware, and as he no doubt expected his listeners to be equally aware, *maʿiyya* may sometimes signify: "escort; suite, retinue, entourage, attendants; the private household of a prince."

best behavior for His sake. Be aware that you are a servant in every situation, while He is a Lord. At every instant and in every state of affairs, the Lord of Truth (Almighty and Glorious is He) is observing our secret thoughts as well as our outwardly visible behavior, so whenever He sees that a heart is loyally devoted to Him, He keeps it safe from the hammer blows of misfortune and the misleading influences of temptation." You need to understand this well, and take it to heart!

The Prophet (Allāh bless him and give him peace) also said:

> Pay careful attention to Allāh and He will take good care of you *[iḥfaẓi 'llāha yaḥfaẓ-ka]*. Pay careful attention to Allāh and you will find Him. When you have a request to make, put your request to Allāh. When you need to ask for help, ask Allāh to help you.[26]

If you put this advice into practice, your behavior will be in accordance with the proper manners of togetherness *[ādāb al-maʿiyya]*. You will be screened by this from the influence of your lower self *[nafs]*, and you will attain to the high stations of spiritual development.

As he [Walī Raslān] (may Allāh be well pleased with him) has said: **"When you are with Him, He screens you from you, and when you are with you, He screens you from Him."**[27] In other words, if you are

[26] As reported by Ibn ʿAbbās (may Allāh be well pleased with him and his father), this *ḥadīth* continues:

> The pen has already run dry from writing all that is to be, so if His servants were to strive to bring you some benefit not decreed for you by Allāh, they would not be capable of it, and if His servants were to strive to cause you some injury not decreed for you by Allāh, they would not be able to do it. So if you can relate to Allāh with honesty and certitude *[yaqīn]*, do so; and if you cannot, there is much good in being patient with what you dislike. Know that help resides in patience, joy with sorrow, and "with hardship comes ease." (Q. 94:5).

In the Forty-second discourse of *Revelations of the Unseen [Futūḥ al-Ghaib]*, Shaikh ʿAbd al-Qādir al-Jīlānī (may Allāh be well pleased with him) remarks:

> It behooves every believer to make this *ḥadīth* a mirror for his heart, to wear it as his undergarment and his outer garb, to treat it as his own *ḥadīth*, on which he should act in all conditions, be he in motion or at rest, so that he may be safe in this world and the hereafter, and receive honor in both domains through the mercy of Allāh (Almighty and Glorious is He).

[27] ***idhā kunta maʿa-hu ḥajabaka ʿan-ka: wa idhā kunta maʿa-ka ḥajabaka ʿan-hu.***

The wording of this particular quotation from the *Risāla* of Walī Raslān is significantly different from the version cited by Zakariyyā' al-Anṣārī in his *Kitāb Fatḥ ar-Raḥmān*. According to the latter, Walī Raslān (may Allāh be well pleased with him) said: **"When you are with Him, He screens you, and when you are with you, He subjects you to serving Him *[idhā kunta maʿa-hu ḥajabaka: wa idhā kunta maʿa-ka 'staʿbadaka la-hu]*."** In his commentary, Zakariyyā' al-Anṣārī adds the words **"from you *[ʿan-ka]*"** after **He screens you,** and his explanation of **He subjects you to serving Him** is: "He makes you a servant devoted to Him *[mutaʿabbidan la-hu]*, for He demands of you service *[ʿibāda]* to Him. This is the state of differentiation *[farq]*, ... in which the individual returns to his formal, outer worship."

present with Him, and if you behave in accordance with the proper manners of togetherness *[ādāb al-maʿiyya]*, He will screen you from you, and the stubbornly reluctant lower self *[an-nafs al-abiyya]*[28] will actually agree to obey you.

Togetherness *[maʿiyya]* has several stages or degrees:

1. At the first stage, you are present with Him in keeping with the standards of behavior proper to the Sacred Law *[ādāb ash-Sharʿ]*. This means that you put into practice what He has commanded you to do, that you avoid what He has forbidden you to do, and that you cheerfully accept what He has decreed and ordained for you. It means that all the limbs and organs of your physical body are actively engaged in worshipful obedience to Him, and that you spend every moment of your time in His service. He will therefore screen you, at this stage, from the distracting influences of your lower self *[nafs]* and your circumstances, and He will enable you to witness His gracious favor toward you.

2. At the intermediate stage, you are present with Him in keeping with the standards of behavior proper to the Spiritual Path *[ādāb aṭ-Ṭarīqa]*. This means that you are personally non-existent in relation to the service in which you are engaged, since there is no work more eagerly hoped for by hearts than the work that has no visible connection with you, and the very existence of which is unimportant from your personal point of view.

As He has said (Exalted is He):

> And the righteous deed He does exalt. (35:10)[29]

[That is to say] He raises it up beyond the notice of the spiritual traveler *[sālik]*, who witnesses nothing in this except the gracious favor of the Sovereign *[Mālik]*.

[28] While the translation "stubbornly reluctant" is probably accurate enough, it fails to convey the whiff of distinctly animal aroma that accompanies the Arabic adjective *abiyya*. As applied to a she-camel, or to any other female beast, *abiyya* means: "reluctant to eat her fodder, by reason of her suffering from indigestion," or, in another context: "unwilling to be covered by the stallion, by reason of her lack of sexual appetite." Since the Arabic word *nafs* [self, esp. the lower self] is grammatically feminine, it lends itself readily to this kind of implied comparison to a reluctant mare or she-camel!

[29] *wa 'l-ʿamalu 'ṣ-ṣāliḥu yarfaʿuh.*

As it has been said: "My God *[Ilāhī]*, if good qualities *[maḥāsin]* appear to come from me, they do so through Your gracious favor, and to You belongs the credit for the kindness bestowed upon me. If evil qualities *[masāwī]* appear, on the other hand, they do so because of Your justice, and to You belongs the evidence against me."

3. At the highest degree, you are present with Him in keeping with the standards of behavior proper to Reality *[ādāb al-Ḥaqīqa]*. This means that you recognize what belongs to you and what belongs to Him, for [the reality is that] to you belong poverty, weakness, incapacity and abject humility, while to Him belong affluence and strength and power and glory. So, if you are present with Him in keeping with these standards of behavior, He will screen your poverty with His affluence, your weakness with His strength, your incapacity with His power, and your abject humility with His glory.

At this stage, therefore, you will witness nothing but His actions *[af'āl]* and His characteristics *[awṣāf]*. Your personal existence *[wujūd]* will fade into insignificance, and every attachment will take its leave of you. The spiritual station of the realization-and-affirmation-of-Oneness *[maqām at-tawḥīd]* will be rightly and properly yours. All that is superfluous *[siwā]* will depart, and you will come to be numbered among the people of singular devotion *[ahl at-tafrīd]*.

How well did that master of wisdom *[ṣāḥib al-ḥukm]* express himself when he said, in reference to these stages or degrees: "The rays of insight *[shi'ā' al-baṣīra]* will cause you to witness His nearness to you. The eye of insight *['ain al-baṣīra]* will cause you to witness your non-existence in relation to His existence. The truth of insight *[ḥaqq al-baṣīra]* will cause you to witness His existence, neither your non-existence nor your existence: [In the beginning] there was Allāh and there was nothing with Him, and He is now in the state in which He was [then]."

All these experiences are among the results of togetherness *[ma'iyya]*, of observing the standards of behavior proper to it, conforming to its rules of conduct, and adhering to its basic principles.

How excellent is the saying: "I shall not stop yawning [from fatigue] until you reconcile yourselves to the fact that I have a limp, and give me a friendly reception in spite of my defect and my imperfection. If you are ready and willing [to accept me on these terms], how splendid for me, how glorious for me! But even if you are unwilling to do so, I shall not be put off by stubborn resistance."

If someone does not merely fail to observe the standards of behavior proper to togetherness [with the Lord] *[ādāb al-ma'iyya]*, but keeps company with his own lower self *[nafs]* instead, following it obediently wherever it happens to lead him, that person is screened from his Master *[Mawlā]* by his own lower self, and it is the most seriously obstructive of all screens.

As Dhu 'n-Nūn[30] (may Allāh be well pleased with him) once put it: "The most seriously obstructive screen, and the hardest to detect, is attention paid to the lower self *[ru'yat an-nafs]* and its schemes."

Besides, the Prophet (Allāh bless him and give him peace) has said:

> None of you will truly believe until his whims and passions *[hawā]* are ready to comply with the message I have brought.

Now that you know this, O my brother, you must desist from obedience to your lower self *[nafs]* and your whims and passions *[hawā]*, and you must part company with your fellow creatures, for then your faith *[īmān]* will become perfect, and your lower self will prove itself capable of dutiful devotion *[taqwā]*. As he [Walī Raslān] (may Allāh be well pleased with him) has said: **"Faith is your separating from them, and certitude is your separating from you."**[31]

[30] Dhu 'n-Nūn Abu 'l-Faiḍ (or Fayyāḍ) Thawbān ibn Ibrāhīm al-Miṣrī was born at Ikhmīm in Upper Egypt, c. A.H. 180 / 796 C.E., the son of a Nubian father. His life is shrouded in obscurity, in spite of the many legends related about him in detailed biographies by later authors. It can be stated with a fair degree of certainty, however, that he lived in Cairo, and that he traveled extensively. We also know that he was arrested (like Imām Aḥmad ibn Ḥanbal) for upholding the traditional Islāmic doctrine that the Qur'ān is uncreated, in opposition to the Mu'tazilite thesis that was espoused by some of the 'Abbāsid Caliphs. He was transported to Baghdād, released after a term of imprisonment, and returned to die at Gīza near Cairo in A.H. 245 / 859 C.E. According to A.J. Arberry (art. DHU 'L-NŪN in *Shorter Encyclopedia of Islam*):

> His sayings display the same intensity of style and rich imagery which character such other [Islāmic saints] as Junaid and Abū Yazīd al-Bisṭāmī. His skill in epigrams is illustrated by the saying: "Make yourself dead during the days of your lifetime, that you may live among the dead when you are gone."

[31] ***al-īmānu khurūju-ka 'an-hum wa 'l-yaqīnu khurūju-ka 'an-ka.*** In Zakariyyā' al-Anṣārī's *Kitāb Fatḥ ar-Raḥmān*, there is one significant difference in the words attributed at this point to the author of the *Risāla*, namely, ***'an-hu* [from Him]** instead of ***'an-hum* [from them]**. The commentary by Zakariyyā' reads:

Perfect **faith *[al-īmān]* is your separating from Him** (Exalted is He) by not associating Him with anything belonging to your personal attributes, **and certitude**

The real meaning of faith *[ḥaqīqat al-īmān]* is the reality of "There is no god but Allāh *[lā ilāha illa 'llāh]*," and when the reality thereof has firmly taken root in someone's heart, that person does not witness any action by anyone other than Him. How then could it be otherwise, for someone who sees with this kind of vision, and is fully aware of its significance, than that he should separate from his fellow creatures and advance toward his Master *[Mawlā]*?

Once he has well and truly arrived at this doorway, and has fulfilled the prerequisites of proper conduct, he will be granted the honor of entry into the house of the loving friends *[manzil al-aḥbāb]*. The goblets of certitude *[yaqīn]* will then be passed around to him, and from them he will sip the choicest beverage of all. Then he will separate from his lower self *[nafs]* and from his own bad attributes. The characteristics of his Master *[Mawlā]* will be conferred upon him, and he will really experience the lofty spiritual stations.

He does not rely with his innermost being *[sirr]* on any other than his Master, and it is only to extol His nobility that he behaves with meekness and humility. Since he is heedful of Allāh with his outer being *[ẓāhir]*, He takes good care of his inner being *[bāṭin]*. Thus he finds Him face to face with him, and this is his greatest wish and desire. As the Prophet (Allāh bless him and give him peace) has told us:

> Pay careful attention to Allāh and He will take good care of you. Pay careful attention to Allāh and you will find Him face to face with you.[32]

How then could it be otherwise, for a person who has attained to the station of face-to-face encounter and direct witnessing *[maqām al-muwājaha wa 'sh-shuhūd]*, than that he should move away from creatures and the lower self *[nafs]*? Once the connection has been made, how could it be exchanged for disconnection?

As somebody once said: "I left my nocturnal pleasure and my happiness in a certain house, and headed back toward the company of a former residence. But the feelings of longing *[ashwāq]* cried out to me: 'Not so fast, for this is the home of someone you are very fond of. Take it easy!'"

[al-yaqīn] is your separating from you, that is, from your own might, your own strength and your own existence, to witness the perfection of His might, His strength and His existence in place of your impotence and weakness.

32 *iḥfaẓi 'llāha yaḥfaẓ-ka: iḥfaẓi 'llāha tajid-hu tujāha-ka.*

You must therefore desist, O my brother, from pointlessly directing your aspiration to any other than Him, for the hopes and expectations of those who apply [to Him] do not escape the notice of the All-Generous One *[al-Karīm]*.

Make sure that your faith *[īmān]* and your certitude *[yaqīn]* are genuinely sound, for then you will be numbered among those who acquire knowledge through direct experience *[ʿārifīn]*. The more deeply rooted in faith you become, the more you will go through transformation in the realm of spiritual states *[aḥwāl]*, and the more deeply rooted in certitude you become, the more you will go through transformation in the realm of spiritual stations *[maqāmāt]*. You will come to possess the character of perfectly developed people *[ahl al-kamāl]*.

As he [Walī Raslān] (may Allāh be well pleased with him) has said: **"When your faith has increased, you will be transported from state to state; and when your certitude has increased, you will be transported from station to station."**[33]

That is to say, when your faith *[īmān]* has increased in strength and deep-rootedness, you will be transported from state to state, and you will come to be one of the experts on the subject of spiritual states *[ahl al-aḥwāl]*; and when your certitude *[yaqīn]* has likewise increased, you will be transported from station to station, and you will come to be one of the experts on the subject of completely developed human beings *[ahl ar-rijāl]*.

The stages entered into by the spiritual traveler *[sālik]* are experienced initially as spiritual states *[aḥwāl]*. Then, once he is firmly rooted and securely established in them, they become a spiritual station *[maqām]* and a complete fulfillment *[kamāl]* for him. You must therefore commit yourself, O my brother, to a noble aspiration, so that you may progress beyond the spiritual states and attain to the lofty spiritual stations.

You can only complete this process of development by constant adherence to the standards of behavior proper to the Sacred Law *[Sharīʿa]*, and by donning the garments appropriate to the Spiritual Path *[Ṭarīqa]*, so that the Reality *[Ḥaqīqa]* may manifest itself to you and

[33] ***idhā zāda īmānu-ka nuqilta min ḥāl ilā ḥāl—wa idhā zāda yaqīnu-ka nuqilta min maqām ilā maqām.***

shine its radiant lights upon you. This is just as he [Walī Raslān] (may Allāh bestow His mercy upon him) has indicated:

"The Sacred Law is for you, until you seek Him from Him for you; and the Reality belongs to Him (Exalted is He), until you seek Him through Him for Him (Almighty and Glorious is He), beyond when and beyond where, for the sacred law does have limits and modes, but the reality has neither limit nor mode."[34]

The point of this reference to the Sacred Law *[Sharī'a]*, and what the statement about it implies, is [that you must surely be aware of] the benefits that will accrue to you [from adhering to it], O spiritual traveler, since the aspiration of the faithful follower of the Sacred Law, and the desired object he has in view, is the bliss of the Garden of Paradise and the pleasures contained therein. This is a prospect of delightful good fortune, which is why he [Walī Raslān (may Allāh be well pleased with him)] has said: "The Sacred Law is for you *[ash-Sharī'a la-ka]*." He has used the Arabic preposition *la-* [for],[35] which indicates that the Sacred Law is a source of benefit for its faithful adherent.

The aim of the faithful adherent of the Sacred Law is to seek the truth from the Lord of Truth *[al-ḥaqq min al-Ḥaqq]*, but not for the sake of his Master *[Mawlā]*. This is why he [Walī Raslān (may Allāh be well pleased with him)] has said: "...until you seek Him (that is, the Lord of Truth) for you (that is, so that this quest will be a benefit accruing to you)."

Meanwhile, "the Reality *[Ḥaqīqa]* belongs to Him," that is, to the Lord of Truth (Exalted is He), "until you seek Him," that is, the Lord of Truth (Exalted is He), "through Him," that is, through the Lord of Truth (Exalted is He), "for Him," that is, also for the sake of the Lord of Truth (Exalted is He), "beyond when and beyond where," since the Lord of Truth (Glorified is He) is not to be qualified in terms of time and space. When and where can only be relevant to someone whose existence is confined to a particular place and a particular time, and Allāh is Exalted very far and beyond anything of the kind!

[34] ***ash-Sharī'a la-ka ḥattā taṭluba-hu min-hu la-ka—wa 'l-Ḥaqīqa la-hu (ta'ālā) ḥattā taṭluba-hu bi-hi la-hu ('azza wa jall) ḥaithu lā ḥīn wa lā ain—fa-'sh-Sharī'a la-hā ḥudūd wa jihāt wa 'l-Ḥaqīqa lā ḥadd wa lā jiha.***

[35] Literally, "he has used the [Arabic letter called] *lām*." Since the short vowels are generally unmarked in an Arabic text, the preposition *la-* appears simply as the consonant *l-* prefixed to the pronoun *-ka* (of which only the consonant *-k* is visible in the text).

This is why he [Walī Raslān (may Allāh be well pleased with him)] has said: "The Sacred Law *[Sharīʿa]* does have limits and modes," because it is limited and dependent upon limitation, "but the Reality *[Ḥaqīqa]* has neither limit nor modes," because it is dependent on the Lord of Truth (Exalted is He), and He (Glorified is He) is entirely exempt from any such qualification.

To put the matter in a nutshell, the Sacred Law *[Sharīʿa]* is [sufficient for the seeker while he is still] at the stage of the boon-companionship of loving friends *[munādamat al-aḥbāb]*.

Then, provided the seeker sticks close to the door, and cultivates good behavior, the faculty of conscience *[sarīra]* will become manifest to him, the faculty of insight *[baṣīra]* will be illuminated for him, and his aspiration will rise far above all inferior goals and purposes. He will be drawn toward lofty pursuits by the attraction of Divine Providence *[al-ʿInāya al-Ilāhiyya]*, to the point where he makes his entrance, through Divine Grace *[al-Faḍl al-Ilāhī]*, into the corridor leading to the Spiritual Path *[Ṭarīqa]*. After that, his further progress will bring him to the stage of the Reality *[Ḥaqīqa]*.

This is why Shaikh Abū ʿAbd al-Qurashī (may Allāh be well pleased with him) once said: "Practice good manners at all times, always do your utmost in the line of servitude *[ʿubūdiyya]*, and never raise objections to anything, for, if you are intent on serving Him, He will connect you with Him."

Well then, O my brother, you must practice at all times the good manners of servitude to your Master *[Mawlā]*, and cast yourself down in humble prostration before Him, for privilege may be granted to both adherents—to the adherent of the Sacred Law *[Sharīʿa]* as well as to the adherent of the Reality *[Ḥaqīqa]*. As he [Walī Raslān] (may Allāh be well pleased with him) has said:

"One who lives with[36] the Sacred Law [alone][37] is given the privilege of striving, and one who lives with the Reality is given the privilege

[36] In his *Kitāb Fatḥ ar-Raḥmān*, Zakariyyāʾ al-Anṣārī prefers the reading *al-qā'im bi…* [one who lives by…], although he does mention that *al-qā'im maʿa…* [one who lives with…] occurs in one copy of the *Risāla* (twice in this quotation).

[37] The word *faqaṭ* [alone] is missing from the quotation given here by al-Ḥamawī, although it appears in the version cited by Zakariyyāʾ al-Anṣārī.

of grace. How great is the contrast between striving and grace!"[38]

That is to say, the business of one who lives with the Sacred Law *[Sharīʿa]* is based on striving and service, since he is at the initial stage, while the business of one who lives with the Reality *[Ḥaqīqa]* is based on pure grace and constant service, since he is at the ultimate stage. And how great is the contrast—that is to say, how great is the distance—between the station of striving *[maqām al-mujāhada]* and the station of grace *[maqām al-minna]*! The person who is committed to striving is immersed in separation, and he is kept behind a screen *[maḥjūb]* by the activity in which he is involved, while the other, being immersed in grace, is beloved *[maḥbūb]* in all his phases of movement and rest.

If he [the loved one] makes a verbal statement, he does so because of Allāh; if he performs an action, he does so for the sake of Allāh; if he comes back from somewhere, it is from Allāh; and if he goes off somewhere, it is toward Allāh; for he is entirely because of Allāh *[bi-'llāh]*, for the sake of Allāh *[li'llāh]*, from Allāh *[mina'llāh]*, and toward Allāh *[ila 'llāh]*. He is not aware of anything but Allāh, and he does not witness anything but Allāh. As it has been said: "Once someone has become truly aware *[ʿarafa]* of Allāh, he witnesses Him in everything." He therefore has no reason to feel alienated from anything, and everything is disposed to treat him in a friendly fashion, for he has come to experience personally—as a normal aspect of nature *[sajiyyatan]* and as an actual fact *[ḥaqīqatan]*—the meaning of the words of Allāh (Exalted is He):

> So whichever way you turn, there is the Face of Allāh. (2:115)[39]

As a result of this, he acquires an excellent state of conscience *[ṭawiyya]*, for conceived *[munṭawiya]* in his heart is [the living reality of the words of Allāh (Exalted is He)]:

> And He is with you wherever you may be. (57:4)[40]

38 ***al-qāʾim maʿa 'sh-sharīʿa [faqaṭ] tafaḍḍala ʿalaihi bi'l-mujāhada—wa 'l-qāʾim maʿa 'l-ḥaqīqa tafaḍḍala ʿalaihi bi'l-minna—wa-shattāna mā baina 'l-mujāhada wa 'l-minna.***

39 *fa-aynamā tuwallū fa-thamma wajhu 'llāh.*

40 *wa Huwa maʿakum ainamā kuntum.*

You must therefore make a very serious effort, O my brother, to place reliance on the gracious favor [of the Lord]. You must pass beyond your personal qualities *[awṣāf]* and make an exit from your personal existence *[wujūd]*, for then you may come to be extinct *[mafqūd]*, or it may be that gracious favors will adorn you. As he [Walī Raslān] (may Allāh be well pleased with him) has said: **"One who lives with striving is existent, while one who lives with grace is extinct."**[41]

The reason for this is that one who lives with striving is always keeping his attention focused on a struggle, always concentrating on what he is trying to do, and on his ability to do it. He is therefore existent in terms of his existence in the realm of fantasy *[mawjūd li-wujūdihi 'l-wahmī]*, and deluded by the shadow that gives him his conventional form *[maghrūr bi-ẓalālihi 'r-rasmī]*.

In the instance of one who lives by grace, on the other hand, no struggle on his part can be observed. No actions are apparent, no power and strength, and nothing in the way of changing states, for he is extinct *[mafqūd]*, nonexistent *[fān]*, wholly immersed in his nonexistence *[fanā᾿]*. He has already been divested of both the two realms of being *[al-kawnain]*, and not a single remnant remains within him—apart from his Master *[Mawlā]*—because he has traversed all the stages *[manāzil]* and states *[aḥwāl]* of spiritual development. He drank from all the springs and pools along the way, until he quenched his thirst with the thirst-quenching draught of the people of perfection *[ahl al-kamāl]*.

Of the practices *[a῾māl]* connected with the Sacred Law *[Shar῾]*, he has accomplished the most lofty; of the states of being *[aḥwāl]* connected with absolute trust in the Lord *[tawakkul]*, he has experienced the most nobly elevated; and of the realization-and-affirmation-of-Oneness *[tawḥīd]* connected with illuminating disclosure *[kashf]*, he has attained to an extremely advanced degree. This relates to what he [Walī Raslān] (may Allāh be well pleased with him) was referring when he said:

"Practices are linked to the noble Law. As for total trust in the Lord, this is linked to faith, and the realization-and-affirmation-of-Oneness is linked to illuminating disclosure."[42]

[41] ***al-qā᾿im ma῾a 'l-mujāhada mawjūd—wa 'l-qā᾿im ma῾a 'l-minna mafqūd.***

[42] ***al-a῾māl muta῾alliqa bi-'sh-Shar῾ ash-sharīf—wa 't-tawakkul muta῾alliq bi-'l-īmān—wa 't-tawḥīd muta῾alliq bi-'l-kashf.*** (As cited by Zakariyyā᾿ al-Anṣārī in his *Kitāb Fatḥ ar-Raḥmān*, this quotation ends with the more vividly explicit expression ***bi-kashf al-ghiṭā*** **[to the removal of the veil].)**

That is to say, the experience of practices *[maʿrifat al-aʿmāl]* is connected with the Sacred Law *[Sharʿ]*, because the latter is the doorway. Unless the seeker steps up to the doorway, he will never enjoy the good fortune of joining the ranks of the loving friends *[aḥbāb]*.

You must therefore be prepared, O spiritual traveler *[sālik]*, to powder your cheek with the dust of the doorsteps of the Sacred Law *[aʿtāb ash-Sharīʿa]*, and to anoint your eyes with the perfection of the manners appropriate to the Spiritual Path *[ādāb aṭ-Ṭarīqa]*. The radiant lights of the Reality *[anwār al-Ḥaqīqa]* will then manifest themselves for your benefit, and you will be able to enjoy the vision of its subtle meanings.

As for total trust in the Lord *[tawakkul]*, it is connected with faith *[īmān]* by virtue of what it really signifies, namely, the fact that contentment with Allāh's knowledge *[ʿilm]* about you is sufficient to release the heart from attachment to anything apart from Him. This state of being is actually attainable, but only for one who truly experiences the real meaning of "There is no god but Allāh *[lā ilāha illa 'llāh]*." It is therefore incumbent upon you, O my brother, to prove the soundness of your faith *[īmān]* by dedicating yourself wholly to your Master *[Mawlā]*, and by turning your attention away from everyone apart from Him. You will thereby attain to the station of total trust in the Lord *[maqām at-tawakkul]*, and He will be pleased with you.

As for the realization-and-affirmation-of-Oneness *[tawḥīd]*, it is something that must actually be tasted *[amr dhawqī]*. It can only be experienced through the revelation of the Sublime *[kashf ar-Rabbānī]*. No one may taste as much as a single mouthful of its juice, unless the cups of direct knowledge *[maʿrifa]* have been passed around to him, and he has been granted the opportunity to make quite sure that the vessels are in a state of good repair. You must therefore make sure that the vessels of your heart are in a state of good repair, O you who yearn so ardently for the pouring of the nectar of the realization-and-affirmation-of-Oneness *[raḥīq at-tawḥīd]*. You must make a very serious effort to bring your heart into a state of good repair, for only then will the full meaning of singular devotion *[tafrīd]* become apparent to you.

As Allāh (Exalted is He) has told us:

> And as for those who strive in Our cause, surely We shall guide them to Our paths. (29:69)[43]

[43] *wa 'lladhīna jāhadū fīnā la-nahdiyannahum subulanā.*

If the seeker lacks a strong determination to pursue the path, he will never enjoy the experience of sitting down to rest with the people [of the Lord], and that nectar will never be readily available to him.

> O suitor, Our beauty is such that Our dower is costly indeed for one who would seek Our hand in marriage: A body that always glows, and a spirit that is never dull; eyelids that never taste drowsiness, and a heart that has no room for anyone but Us. So whenever you wish, you have only to pay the price!
>
> Cease to exist, therefore, if you wish for endless nonexistence *[fanāʾan sarmadan]*, for ceasing to exist will lead to such nonexistence. Take off both shoes if you come to that valley, for in it We are sanctified; and of both the two realms of being *[al-kawnain]* let yourself be divested. Set down whatever stands in the way between us, and whenever you are asked, "Whom do you love?" say, "I am the one whom I love *[anā man ahwā anā]*."[44]

This station *[maqām]* is accessible only to someone who is honored with the ability to follow guidance, and who comes to be one of those who are loved *[maḥbūbīn]*. This is someone who acts in accordance with the signs and indications he receives, and who takes steps to correct both the outer *[ẓāhir]* and the inner *[bāṭin]* aspects of his being. He comes to be numbered among the inheritors *[wārithīn]*, at which point the true facts *[ḥaqāʾiq]* are disclosed to him, and now he may drink of this pure drink—every crystal clear drop of it *[kulla rāʾiq]*.

As for the kind of person who races into this arena with his mental faculty *[ʿaql]* in control, he will not cease to wander astray in the deserts of confusion. If someone tries to find the Garden of Paradise with the help of his own lower self *[nafs]* and his passions *[hawā]*, he is bound to stray from the path, and he is sure to ignore the blessings and benefits that Allāh has provided to assist him. As he [Walī Raslān] (may Allāh be well pleased with him) has said:

"People wander astray from the Lord of Truth (Exalted is He) because of the mind, and from the hereafter because of passion. For, when you seek the Lord of Truth (Exalted is He) with the mind, you

[44] This passage would seem to be a quotation from the work of a mystic poet. (The original Arabic is rhymed, and—as far as it is possible to judge from the white-on-black photocopy available to the translator—the manuscript version was written with a different ink from that used to inscribe the main body of the text.)

lose the way, and when you seek the hereafter with passion, you stumble and slip."[45]

The Lord of Truth (Exalted is He) can only be recognized by the light of faith *[nūr al-īmān]*, just as the Garden of Paradise can only be attained through opposition [to the lower self and the passions], and by consistently upright conduct at the station of active goodness *[maqām al-iḥsān]*. If someone tries to observe the Reality *[Ḥaqīqa]* with the eye of his mental faculty *[ʿaql]*, he will therefore remain in a state of disconnection *[tafarraqa]*, while he who looks for it by light of faith will enjoy the real experience *[taḥaqqaqa]*. The most useful purpose the mind can serve is to show you how to reach the doorway. As for the first [stage of the journey from that point on] toward the Divine Presence *[Ḥaḍra]*, there is no way to embark upon it except through constant cultivation of the appropriate modes of behavior *[ādāb]*.

As he [the Prophet] (Allāh bless him and give him peace) has told us:

> Pay careful attention to Allāh and He will take good care of you. Pay careful attention to Allāh and you will find Him face to face with you.[46]

That is to say, you must pay careful attention to Allāh by constantly cultivating the appropriate modes of behavior, for you will thereby gain access to the station of meeting face to face *[maqām al-muwājaha]*, and you will come to be numbered among the loving friends *[aḥbāb]*. The station of direct experience *[maqām al-muwājaha]* can only be attained by following in the footsteps of the loving friend *[ḥabīb]*, so if a seeker tries to find it by using his mind, he will fail to obtain any share *[naṣīb]* in the object of his quest. By the same token, the Garden of Paradise can only be attained through opposition to the lower self *[nafs]* and the passions *[hawā]*, so if a seeker tries to find it by any other means, he is shooting wide of the mark.

As Allāh (Exalted is He) has told us:

> But as for him who feared to stand before his Lord, and forbade the lower self to follow passion, surely the Garden [of Paradise] will be his final place of rest. (79:40,41)[47]

[45] ***an-nās tā'ihūn ʿani 'l-Ḥaqq (taʿālā) bi-'l-ʿaql—wa ʿani 'l-ākhira bi-'l-hawā—fa-matā ṭalabta 'l-Ḥaqq (taʿālā) bi-'l-ʿaql ḍalalta—wa matā ṭalabta 'l-ākhira bi-'l-hawā ẓalalta.***

[46] *iḥfaẓi 'llāha yaḥfaẓ-ka: iḥfaẓi 'llāha tajid-hu tujāha-ka.*

[47] *wa ammā man khāfa maqāma Rabbi-hi wa naha 'n-nafsa ʿani 'l-hawā—fa-inna 'l-jannata hiya 'l-maʾwā.*

It is therefore incumbent upon you, O my brother, to dedicate yourself to acts of worshipful obedience *[ṭāʿāt]*, while avoiding all acts of sinful disobedience *[maʿāṣī]*. You must always observe those religious duties that are strictly obligatory *[farāʾiḍ]*, and you must also acquire merit through the performance of supererogatory devotions *[nawāfil]* at all times, so that you may gain access to the station of the Garden of Paradise *[maqām al-Janna]*, so that the light of faith *[nūr al-īmān]* may shine in your heart, so that you may experience the feeling of rapture *[jadhba]*, and so that direct knowledge *[maʿrifa]* may pervade your entire being. You will then behold Him by it [by His light], and gracious favor will envelop you completely, even when you are neither standing still [in His presence] nor prostrating yourself before Him.

As he [Walī Raslān] (may Allāh be well pleased with him) has said: **"The believer sees by the light of Allāh, and one who has direct knowledge beholds Him by it."**[48]

The believer *[muʾmin]* sees by the light of Allāh because he is still at the initial stage, while one who has direct knowledge *[ʿārif]* beholds Him by it because he is at the ultimate stage. The believer *[muʾmin]* is someone from whom the dark shadows of polytheistic association *[shirk]* have vanished away, and for whom the radiant lights have begun to shine. As for the person who knows by direct experience *[ʿārif]*, he is someone who has ceased to exist in relation to his lower self *[nafs]* and his personal characteristics *[awṣāf]*, so he witnesses nothing but his Master *[Mawlā]*, and all others have disappeared from his sight.

The truth of the first statement [the one concerning the believer] is borne out by his [the Prophet's] words (Allāh bless him and give him peace):

> Beware of the penetrating insight of the believer, for he sees by the light of his Lord.[49]

As for the second statement, we may cite his words (Allāh bless him and give him peace) as they occur in the following Sacred Tradition *[Ḥadīth Qudsī]*:[50]

> And My servant continues to draw near to Me through supererogatory acts of worship *[nawāfil]* until I love him; and when I love him, I come to be his hearing by which he hears, and his eyesight by which he sees.[51]

[48] ***al-muʾmin yanẓuru bi-nūri 'llāh—wa 'l-ʿārif yanẓuru bi-hi ilai-hi.***

[49] *ittaqū firāsata 'l-muʾmin ; fa-inna-hu yanẓuru bi nūri Rabbi-hi.*

This is the farthest point of the station of servitude *[maqām al-ʿubūdiyya]*, and the most splendid of all the qualities of Lordship *[awṣāf ar-Rubūbiyya]* with which the servant may be honorably endowed. You must therefore make quite sure, O servant [of the Lord], that your own qualities are fully realized, for He will then endow you with His qualities. You must humble yourself through your servitude, and be ready to receive the gifts of grace *[nafaḥāt]*, especially at the times of early morning prayer *[awqāt al-fajr]*, for those moments are replete with bountiful blessings *[barakāt]*. This was so very well expressed by the anonymous person who said:

"Endure with patience the agonies of traveling by night, especially in the period just before the break of day, and persevere in acts of worshipful obedience during the early morning time. I have discovered that the days contain a test of patience, a conclusion worthy of being noted and applied."

Few and far between are those who make really serious efforts to complete any business they set out hoping to accomplish, and who take patience along with them as a companion in the process, otherwise there would surely be more stories of success!

You must therefore make a very serious effort, O my brother, to ensure that you truly arrive at the station of faith *[maqām al-īmān]*. In order to do so, you must obey the commandments and avoid any violation of the prohibitions [laid down by the Sacred Law], until you receive the blessing of providential care *[ʿināya]*. Once you have reached that stage, you will be rendered extinct as far as your personal existence is concerned, and you will experience the Divine benevolence *[al-luṭf*

[50] A somewhat longer and slightly different version of this Sacred Tradition *[Ḥadīth Qudsī]* is cited by Shaikh ʿAbd al-Qādir al-Jīlānī (may Allāh be well pleased with him) in the Thirty-ninth Discourse of *The Sublime Revelation [al-Fatḥ ar-Rabbānī]* (p. 252 of the Al-Baz edition):

> Those who draw near do not draw near to Me with anything more excellent than the fulfillment of that which I have established as a duty for them. And My servant continues to draw near to Me through supererogatory acts of worship *[nawāfil]* until I love him; and when I love him, I become for him a hearing and an eyesight, a hand and a support, so through Me he hears, through Me he sees and through Me he grasps.

[51] *wa lā yazālu ʿabdī yataqarrabu ʿalayya bi-'n-nawāfili ḥattā aḥibbahu—fa-idhā aḥbabta-hu kuntu samʿa-hu 'lladhī yasmaʿu bi-hi wa baṣara-hu 'lladhī yabṣuru bi-hi.*

al-Ilāhī] in all its fullness, as indicated by these words of his [of Walī Raslān] (may Allāh be well pleased with him):

"[The Lord says]: 'As long as you are with you, We command you. Then, once you have been rendered extinct to you, We take charge of you.' For He does not take charge of them until after their annihilation [in Him]."[52]

That is to say, as long as you are at the station of separation *[maqām al-farq]*, and while you are still attached to your personal existence *[wujūd]*, We command you, but once you are at the station of integration *[maqām al-jamʿ]*, and have reached the point of complete detachment *[ghaiba]* from everything apart [from the Lord], We take charge of you. In other words, as long as you are still at the initial stage, you are at the station of striving *[maqām al-mujāhada]*, but when you are at the ultimate stage, you are at the station of direct witnessing *[maqām al-mushāhada]*, and once the seeker has witnessed his Master *[Mawlā]* directly, how could he be left with any interest whatsoever in anything apart from Him?

As he [the Prophet] (Allāh bless him and give him peace) has told us:

> And my chief comfort [literally, the cooling of my eye] has been made to reside in the ritual prayer.[53]

For someone who knows by direct experience *[ʿārif]*, every single moment is a time of ritual prayer *[ṣalāt]*, since the essential reality of the ritual prayer *[ḥaqīqat aṣ-ṣalāt]* is turning one's back on everything else *[ʿani 's-siwā]* and turning to face the Master *[ʿalā 'l-Mawlā]*.

Once the seeker has genuinely experienced this direct vision, he will still be involved in his actions from the standpoint of his outer being *[ẓāhir]*, but he will be quite detached from them as far as his heart and his innermost contents *[sarāʾir]* are concerned. This is what actually does happen when the Lord of Truth takes charge of him *[ḥaqīqatu tawallī 'l-Ḥaqqi iyyāhu]*, due to the fact that his physical form *[qālab]* is dedicated to active servitude, while his inner core *[qalb]* is intently beholding the presence of his Master *[ḥaḍrat Mawlāhu]*.

[52] ***mā dumta anta maʿa-ka amarnā-ka—fa-idhā fanaita ʿan-ka tawallainā-ka—fa-mā tawallā-hum illā baʿda fanāʿihim [fī-hi].*** (The words *fī-hi* [in Him] are absent from the quotation provided here by al-Ḥamawī, although they do occur in the version cited by Zakariyyāʾ al-Anṣārī.)

[53] *wa juʿilat qurratu ʿainī fi 'ṣ-ṣalāt.*

It is therefore incumbent upon you, O my brother, to spare no effort in the way of service, and to cast yourself down in prostration before Him, for thus you may be deemed worthy of acceptance in His presence. Then He may render you extinct to you, and draw you close to Him.

[In the words of Walī Raslān (may Allāh be well pleased with him)]: **"As long as you continue, you are a seeker. Then, when He has made you extinct to you, you are one who is sought."**[54]

That is to say, as long as you continue to attach importance to your own lower self *[nafs]*, and continue to keep it in existence, you are still at the initial stage. Once you have moved to a position of detachment from it, and have experienced its annihilation, only then will you be at the ultimate stage.

The root cause of every sinful act of disobedience, of heedless negligence and of lustful indulgence, is satisfaction with the lower self *[ar-riḍā ʿani 'n-nafs]*, while the root cause of every act of worshipful obedience, of vigilant awareness and of good conscience, is the lack of satisfaction with the lower self *[ʿadam ar-riḍā ʿani 'n-nafs]*—the lack of satisfaction with it on your own part. Satisfaction with the lower self *[nafs]* is the main incentive for keeping it in existence, and satisfaction is fed by admiration of its charming and attractive features. The lack of satisfaction with it, on the other hand, is the main incentive for discarding it, and satisfaction is diminished by focusing attention on its repugnant and disgusting features.

You must therefore take a suspicious view of your own lower self *[nafs]*, O my brother, in all your states and conditions, so that the station of servitude *[maqām al-ʿubūdiyya]* may be truly yours, and so that you may advance to the peak of your perfection. Glory be to the One who has hidden the secret of peculiar distinction *[khuṣūṣiyya]* within the external appearance of humanity *[bashariyya]*, and who manifests Himself through the majesty of Lordship *[Rubūbiyya]* in the demonstration of servitude *[ʿubūdiyya]*!

It is therefore incumbent upon you, O my brother, to practice contrition and humility inside this doorway. You must cast aside reliance on power and strength, for then you may be allowed to experience the most lasting certainty *[al-yaqīn al-adwam]*, and you may

[54] ***mā dumta anta fa-anta murīd—fa-idhā afnā-ka ʿan-ka fa-anta murād.***

acquire the excellent qualities of the loving friends *[shamāʾil al-aḥbāb]*. He [Walī Raslān] (may Allāh be well pleased with him) has said:

"The most lasting certainty is your absence from you and your presence with Him. What a big difference there is between what is at His command and what is because of Him! If you are at His command, worldly means will be subservient to you. And if you are because of Him, the whole Universe will be submissive to you."[55]

That is to say, the certainty *[yaqīn]* on which the people of direct knowledge *[ahl al-maʿrifa]* place their reliance, and the lasting nature of which they verify by the test of experience, is the certainty that is received from Him (Exalted is He), once you have come to be absent from you and present because of Him *[mawjūd bi-hi]*, surrounded by the noble ones *[kirām]*. How great indeed is the difference, therefore, between being at His command, as one of those who are still at the initial stage *[ahl al-bidāya]*, and being because of Him, as one of those who are at the ultimate stage *[ahl an-nihāya]*. If you are at His command, and you master the chapter of striving *[bāb al-mujāhada]*, worldly means *[asbāb]* will be subservient to you. If you are because of Him, and you really and truly attain to the station of extinction *[maqām al-fanāʾ]*, the whole universe will be submissive to you.

To put this entire subject in a nutshell, there is a first step that must be taken by the traveler on the spiritual path, namely, compliance with the [Divine] commandments and nonviolation of the [Divine] prohibitions. To take this step is to step up to the doorway of the Sacred Law *[Sharīʿa]*. Once this door has been opened for him completely, the spiritual traveler will be granted the honor of entry into the dwelling places of the loving friends *[aḥbāb]*. There he must purify himself by getting rid of all his unworthy qualities, at which point he will be dressed in noble attire, for the robes of Honor Sublime *[al-khilaʿ ar-Rabbāniyya]* will then be brought forth. Worldly means *[asbāb]* will thus become subservient to him at the first station, because he has been obedient to Allāh. When someone obeys Him, everything becomes obedient to that person, as we know from what has come down to us in the tradition

[55] ***al-yaqīn al-adwam ghaibatu-ka ʿan-ka wa wujūdu-ka bi-hi—kam baina mā yakūnu bi-amri-hi wa baina mā yakūnu bi-hi—in kunta bi-amri-hi khaḍaʿat la-ka ʾl-asbāb—wa in kunta bi-hi taḍaʿḍaʿat la-ka ʾl-akwān.***

[ḥadīth] concerning the well-known story of Abū Ṭālib[56] [and how the Prophet (Allāh bless him and give him peace) once said to him]:

> And you, uncle, if only you would obey Him, He would obey you! *[wa anta—yā ʿamm—law aṭaʿta-hu la-aṭāʿa-ka].*[57]

Then, at the second station, the whole universe comes to be submissive to him, because he has become extinct to his own lower self *[nafs]*, so that nothing remains within his field of vision apart from his Master *[Mawlā]*. The truth of this assertion is borne out by the words of Allāh (Exalted is He) [addressed to the Prophet (Allāh bless him and give him peace)]:

> And it was not you who did the throwing, when you threw [that handful of dust or sand in battle with the unbelieving foe], but Allāh did the throwing. (8:17)[58]

Once you have grasped the meaning of this, O my brother, you must go on to make real progress through the various stages of the spiritual journey *[sulūk]*. You must apply yourself diligently to the quest, and be careful to make the most of every second of your time, for then you will come to be numbered among the kings *[mulūk]*. As Shaikh Abu 'l-Ḥasan ash-Shādhilī[59] (may Allāh be well pleased with him) once said: "If your purpose is to seek and find the kings of the two domains *[mulūk ad-dārain]*, then embark upon this path *[ṭarīq]* of ours for a day or two!"

You must also realize that you will not be allowed to enjoy the full aroma of a single whiff of the fragrant perfume of this path *[ṭarīq]*, as long as you have not duly traversed the various stations *[maqāmāt]*, and as long as you have not unloaded every impediment *[taʿwīq]* from your heart. [In the words of Walī Raslān (may Allāh be well pleased with him)]:

[56] Abū Ṭālib was the father of Imām ʿAlī (may Allāh be well pleased with him) and uncle of the Prophet (Allāh bless him and give him peace). Although he served his nephew as a guardian and then as a faithful friend for forty years, Abū Ṭālib was a notoriously stubborn character, and he is believed to have died—in the third year before the Hijra—without ever having embraced the religion of Islām.

[57] This saying may strike the reader as rather shocking, and the Prophet (Allāh bless him and give him peace) no doubt intended it to have a startling impact. It should be pointed out, however, that the Arabic verb *aṭāʿa*, while it does commonly mean "to obey," may also convey the less absolute meaning "to accede to a person's wishes" (in answer to a prayer, for instance).

[58] *wa mā ramaita idh ramaita wa lākinna 'llāha ramā.*

[59] See note 8 on p. 41 above.

"The first of the stations is patience in obedience to His will (Exalted is He). **The one in the middle is contentment with His wishes** (Exalted is He), **and the last is that you come to be in accordance with His purpose** (Exalted is He).**"**[60]

That is to say, the first of the stations to be traversed by spiritual travelers *[maqāmāt as-sālikīn]* is that of patience *[ṣabr]* in obedience to the Will of the Lord of Truth.

As somebody once put it: "Patience is the key to all that is hoped for, and every problem is made easier by its application, so it may in fact be possible, through patiently biding one's time, to achieve what people had dismissed as utterly absurd and completely out of the question."[61]

To quote another saying of similar import: "The token of success, in achieving the object sought, is the exercise of patience in fulfilling the wishes of the loved one."[62]

The reward for patience is indeed beyond all reckoning, as Allāh (Exalted is He) has told us:

> Surely those who are patient will be paid their wages in full without reckoning. (39:10)[63]

Once the seeker has well and truly arrived at this [first] station, and provided he has behaved there in a right and proper manner, it will next become appropriate for him to enter the station of contentment *[maqām ar-riḍā]*, and to enjoy its special properties.

This [station of contentment] is the most central *[awsaṭ]* of all the stations, and it is the most equitable *[aʿdal]* of them all. Once he has entered into it, the spiritual traveler will be granted the most excellent opportunities to experience perfection *[mukammilāt]*. How splendid is the saying:[64]

> O you who are content to accept Our judgments, you are certainly bound to praise the outcome of contentment. Entrust your affairs to Us,

[60] ***awwal al-maqāmāt aṣ-ṣabr ʿalā murādi-hi—wa awsaṭu-hā 'r-riḍā—wa ākhiru-hā an takūna bi-murādi-hi.***

[61] *aṣ-ṣabru miftāḥu mā yurjā wa kullu khaṭbin bi-hi yahūn—fa-rubba-mā nīla bi-'t-taʾannī mā qīla haihātu lā yakūn.*

[62] *ʿunwān aẓ-ẓafr bi-'l-maṭlūb at-taḥaqquq ʿalā murādāt al-maḥbūb.*

[63] *innamā yuwaffa 'ṣ-ṣābiruna ajra-hum bi-ghairi ḥisāb.*

[64] Although the author does not say so explicitly, this must surely be a Divine Saying *[Ḥadīth Qudsī]*.

> and continue to be a Muslim [one who submits to the will of Allāh], for the supreme comfort is enjoyed by one who entrusts his affairs to Us. A man will never be fully united with his Beloved, until he experiences bewilderment concerning that which He has decreed.[65]

Once he has mastered the lessons of this station, the seeker will be ready to advance to the ultimate stage. He will become extinct to his own lower self *[nafs]* and to his personal characteristics *[awṣāf]*, and he will reach the final goal. At this point he will be in accordance with the purpose of the Lord of Truth *[murād al-Ḥaqq]*, inasmuch as he is no longer in possession of any self-will *[irāda]*. He will now experience the reality of the station of "through Me he hears and through Me he sees *[maqām bī yasmaʿu wa bī yabṣuru]*," and the radiant lights of this state of bliss will shine upon him.

All of these experiences are among the results to be obtained by constant cultivation of the proper modes of behavior *[ādāb]*, by unceasing remembrance *[dhikr]* practiced with the heart, and by clinging to the dust of the doorsteps *[aʿtāb]*. The remembrance [expressed by repeating the words] "There is no god but Allāh *[lā ilāha illa 'llāh]*" will lead to the point where hearts as well as mouths rejoice in the remembrance of Him.

You must also see to it that your finest decoration is your pious devotion, O brother of the veil *[akhā 'l-ḥijāb]*, for how well deserving is he whose finery is his piety *[ḥulāhu tuqāhu]*! You must put your thoughts to work on the contemplation of His kingdom *[malakūt]*, engrossing yourself in the process of discovering its meaning. You must slip off your shoes [as a mark of respect for hallowed ground], like a genuine explorer *[muḥaqqiq]* who has passed beyond the two realms of being in the course of his journey by night *[masrā]*. You must become extinct even to your own extinction *[fanāʾ]*, for therein is the source of perpetuity *[baqāʾ]*, and at that moment you will see Him. Then, when He has manifested Himself to you, you must be well aware that you are not He *[lasta Huwa]*—by no means!—and also that you are not something apart from Him *[siwāhu]*. Two things do not co-exist [that is, there is no question of dualism]—but here we have a mystery *[sirr]* so profound that it defies our ability to grasp what it really signifies.

65 *yā ayyuha 'r-raḍiyyu bi-aḥkāminā lā budda an taḥmida ʿuqbā 'r-riḍā—fawwiḍ ilainā wa 'bqa muslimā—fa-'r-rāḥatu 'l-ʿuẓmā li-man fawwaḍanā—lā yatimmu 'l- marʾu bi-maḥbūbi-hi ḥattā yara 'l-ḥairata fī-mā qad qaḍā.*

O listener, as I have already tried to make you understand, you cannot experience transformation *[qalb]*[66] by thinking about what you hear and retain with your ears. You must remove the veil, the veil that covers your heart *[qalb]*, for only then will the secret be disclosed to you, revealing the brilliant splendor that was previously invisible to your sight. God is One who is supremely ready to make Himself known *[inna 'l-Ilāha Ajallu mutaʿrrifin]*, so if someone does not see Him, that person must obviously be afflicted with blindness. How could He disappear from view, when nothing exists apart from Him? And yet it is hard indeed to discover anything that He has concealed!

Well then, O you who long so ardently for the attainment of these lofty stations *[maqāmāt]*, and you who are yearning to quench your thirst with a draught from these salutary cups, it is incumbent upon you to learn the real meaning of knowledge *[maʿrifat al-ʿilm]*, and to put that knowledge correctly into practice *[taṣḥīḥ al-ʿamal]*. If you act on this advice, you will succeed in obtaining intimate knowledge *[al-ʿilm al-ladunī]*, and in acquiring direct insight *[maʿrifa]* and revelatory disclosure *[kashf]*. You will become extinct [to your separate personal identity], and you will arrive at your destination together with those who also reach that goal. As he [Walī Raslān] (may Allāh be well pleased with him) has said:

"[Practical] knowledge is the way of action, and action is [the way of] knowledge. And knowledge is the way of experience. And experience [of Allāh] is the way of unveiling. And unveiling is the way of extinction."[67]

66 When it represents the verbal noun corresponding to the Arabic verb *qalaba*, the word *qalb* means "turning around; transformation." It is much more common, however, as an ordinary noun, derived from the same triconsonantal root, *q-l-b*. In the latter case (an example of which occurs in the second sentence of the passage to which this note refers), the meaning of *qalb* is "heart; inner core."

67 ***al-ʿilm [al-ʿamalī] ṭarīq al-ʿamal—wa 'l-ʿamal [ṭarīq] al-ʿilm—wa 'l-ʿilm ṭarīq al-maʿrifa—wa 'l-maʿrifa [bi-'llāh] ṭarīq al-kashf—wa 'l-kashf ṭarīq al-fanāʾ.*** (The words enclosed between brackets are omitted from the text of al-Ḥamawī's commentary on the Risāla, although they do occur in the version quoted by Zakariyyāʾ al-Anṣārī. It should also be noted that al-Ḥamawī completely omits the sentence which follows at this point in the version quoted by Zakariyyāʾ al-Anṣārī, namely: **"extinction is a matter of action, then of essence, then of reality"** ***[wa 'l-fanāʾ yakūnu ʿamalan, thumma ʿainan, thumma ḥaqqan]***.)

That is to say, knowledge of the Sacred Law and of the Spiritual Path *[al-ʿilm bi-'sh-Sharīʿa wa 'ṭ-Ṭarīqa]* is the way of action *[ṭarīq al-ʿamal]*, while action in conformity with both of them is the way of intimate knowledge *[ṭaʿrīq al-ʿilm al-ladunī]*. As Allāh (Exalted is He) has told us:

> Be dutiful toward Allāh, and Allāh will teach you. (2:282)[68]

And as he [the Prophet] (Allāh bless him and give him peace) has said:

> When someone puts what he knows into practice, Allāh makes him heir to knowledge of what he did not know.[69]

Intimate knowledge *[al-ʿilm al-ladunī]* is the way of direct experience *[ṭarīq al-maʿrifa]*, since the servant cannot know his Master *[Mawlā]* directly except through His granting him direct experience of Himself *[illā bi-taʿrīfihi iyyāhu]*. Once the servant has come to know Him through this direct experience, the real facts *[ḥaqāʾiq]* will be disclosed to him, he will become extinct to everything else [apart from his Master], and he will drink from the cups of the sources of pure wine *[khamr rāʾiq]*.

The main point to be emphasized here is that it is absolutely necessary for the spiritual wayfarer *[sālik]* to acquire direct experience of the Sacred Law and of the Spiritual Path *[maʿrifat ash-Sharīʿa wa 'ṭ-Ṭarīqa]*, and to do so at the very beginning of his journey, so that he may use them both as his means of transport across the desolate tracts of the desert wastes, and thus arrive at his ultimate destination. You must therefore be sure to equip yourself, O traveler journeying toward the [Divine] Presence *[Ḥaḍra]*, with the most suitable means of transport and the most convenient accessories you can muster. You must also take great pains to ensure that no remnants of worldly attachments are still clinging to you.

[According to Walī Raslān (may Allāh be well pleased with him), the Lord says]:

"You have not become fit for Us as long as there is still within you any remnant of anything apart from Us, so when you have set everything else aside, We shall render you extinct. You have now become fit for Us, and We have entrusted you with Our secret."[70]

[68] *wa 'ttaqu 'llāh—wa yuʿallimu-kumu 'llāh.*

[69] *man ʿamila bi-mā ʿalima warratha-hu 'llāhu ʿilma mā lam yaʿlam.*

[70] ***mā ṣalaḥta la-nā mā dāmat fī-ka baqiyya li-siwā-nā—fa-idhā ḥawwalta 's-siwā afnainā-ka ʿan-ka—wa-ṣalaḥta la-nā wa-awdaʿnā-ka sirranā.*** (The version quoted by Zakariyyāʾ al-Anṣārī reads: ***fa-ṣalaḥta la-nā fa-awdaʿnā-ka sirranā.***)

Al-Junaid[71] (may Allāh be well pleased with him) once said: "The *mukātab* is a slave *[ʿabd]* as long as he still owes a single dirham [silver coin]."[72] The very same principle applies in the case of the spiritual wayfarer *[sālik]*, for, as long as he still pays any attention to anything apart from his Master *[Mawlā]*, and as long as he remains in any way attached to his worldly fortune and pleasures, he is not yet fit to enter the presence of His exalted majesty. Once everything else has gone out of his heart, and nothing remains within it apart from his Master, at that point his Master will come to his aid. He will render him extinct to himself, make him fit for His presence, and entrust the secret to him, so he will come to be an example for others to learn from and to follow.

This is why somebody once said: "The path is actually two paths *[aṭ-ṭarīq ṭarīqān]*: the path of those who proceed at a moderate pace *[ṭarīq al-muqtaṣidīn]*, and the path of the bold explorers *[ṭarīq al-muḥaqqiqīn]*. The path of those who proceed at a moderate pace consists of fasting *[ṣiyām]*, keeping vigil *[qiyām]*, and giving up sins *[tark al-āthām]*. The path of the bold explorers, on the other hand, is the route of migration away from all creatures *[khalāʾiq]*, of severing all worldly attachments *[ʿalāʾiq]*, and of strenuous exertion in the service of the Creator *[Khāliq]*. This is the distinction indicated by Shaikh ʿAbd al-Qādir al-Gīlānī[73] (may Allāh be well pleased with him), when he says:

"O my brothers, I did not attain to Allāh by keeping vigil through the night, nor by fasting through the day, nor yet by the study of academic knowledge *[ʿilm]*. But I did attain to Allāh by way of noblehearted generosity *[karam]*, modest humility *[tawāḍuʿ]*, and soundness of the feeling within the breast *[salāmat aṣ-ṣadr]*."

[71] Abu 'l-Qāsim ibn Muḥammad ibn al-Junaid al-Khazzāz al-Qawārīrī an-Nihāwandī (d. A.H. 298/910 C.E.). The son of a glass-merchant and nephew of Sarī as-Saqaṭī, he was a close associate of al-Muḥāsibī. Renowned for the clarity of his perception and the firmness of his self-control, he earned a reputation as the principal exponent of the "sober" school of Islāmic mysticism. His *Rasāʾil* [Epistles] consist of letters to private individuals, and short tractates on mystical themes, some cast in the form of commentaries on Qurʾānic texts.

[72] A *mukātab* is a slave who has made a written contract with his master, in which it is stipulated that the slave will be granted his freedom on the payment of a certain sum. As al-Junaid (may Allāh be well pleased with him) points out, that sum must be paid in full before the *mukātab* becomes a free man.

[73] The Arabic letter *kāf* is used in this spelling of the name, suggesting the Persian pronunciation, as opposed to the more usual Arabic form "al-Jīlānī", which is spelled with the initial letter *jīm*. (The hard sound "g"—as in the English word "go"—does not occur in normal Arabic, although it is common in the Persian language, where the

It is indeed by way of noblehearted generosity that the spiritual traveler *[sālik]* moves beyond attachment to this world. It is indeed by way of modest humility that he moves beyond attachment to the lower self *[nafs]*, and it is indeed through soundness of the inner feeling that he moves beyond attachment to everything else, so that he is left with no interest in anything but the Master *[Mawlā]*. This is the ultimate goal of those who know directly by experience *[al-ʿārifīn]*, and the final object of those who are the heirs to empowerment *[al-wārithīn li't-tamkīn]*.

It is therefore incumbent upon you, O my brother, to ensure that you are truly fit and worthy of this station. You must abandon your self-motivated undertakings, and become extinct to your personal existence, for then you will be granted certainty *[yaqīn]*, your realization-and-affirmation-of-Oneness *[tawḥīd]* will be perfected, and you will be allowed to drink this pure wine *[mudām]*. As he [Walī Raslān] (may Allāh be well pleased with him) has said:

"When there does not remain with you any self-motivation, your

extra letter *gāf*, formed by placing a bar over the Arabic letter *kāf*, has been added to the alphabet.)

Through the mists of legend surrounding the life of Shaikh ʿAbd al-Qādir al-Jīlānī (may Allāh be well pleased with him), it is possible to discern the outlines of the following biographical sketch:

In A.H. 488, at the age of eighteen, he left his native province to become a student in the great capital city of Baghdād, the hub of political, commercial and cultural activity, and the center of religious learning in the world of Islām. After studying traditional sciences under such teachers as the prominent Ḥanbalī jurist *[faqīh]*, Abū Saʿd ʿAlī al-Mukharrimī, he encountered a more spiritually oriented instructor in the saintly person of Abu'l-Khair Ḥammād ad-Dabbās. Then, instead of embarking on his own professorial career, he abandoned the city and spent twenty-five years as a wanderer in the desert regions of ʿIrāq. He was over fifty years old by the time he returned to Baghdād, in A.H. 521/1127 C.E., and began to preach in public. His hearers were profoundly affected by the style and content of his lectures, and his reputation grew and spread through all sections of society. He moved into the school *[madrasa]* belonging his old teacher al-Mukharrimī, but the premises eventually proved inadequate. In A.H. 528, pious donations were applied to the construction of a residence and guesthouse *[ribāṭ]*, capable of housing the Shaikh and his large family, as well as providing accommodation for his pupils and space for those who came from far and wide to attend his regular sessions *[majālis]*. He lived to a ripe old age, and continued his work until his very last breath, as we know from the accounts of his final moments recorded in the Addendum to Revelations of the Unseen.

In the words of Shaikh Muzaffer Ozak Efendi: "The venerable ʿAbd al-Qādir al-Jīlānī passed on to the Realm of Divine Beauty in A.H. 561/1166 C.E., and his blessed mausoleum in Baghdād is still a place of pious visitation. He is noted for his extraordinary spiritual experiences and exploits, as well as his memorable sayings and wise teachings. It is rightly said of him that 'he was born in love, grew in perfection, and met his Lord in the perfection of love.' May the All-Glorious Lord bring us in contact with his lofty spiritual influence!"

certitude will be perfected, and when there does not remain any existence of yours, your realization-and-affirmation-of-Oneness will be perfected."[74]

That is to say, when you are no longer subject to the influence of any self-motivation *[ḥaraka li-nafsi-ka]*, this will indicate your recognition of the fact that the One who causes both movement and rest *[al-Muḥarrik wa 'l-Musakkin]* is actually your Master *[Mawlā]*. Once you have truly experienced this, He will regard you as worthy of Him. Once you are left without any personal existence—since you have become extinct to you—the realization-and-affirmation-of-Oneness *[tawḥīd]* will be complete, and you will come to be numbered among the people of perfection *[ahl al-kamāl]*. Your standing will then be implicity accepted by all.

The substitution of stillness for movement constitutes the doorway, and your passing beyond your personal existence *[wujūd]*—through the perfection of your realization-and-affirmation-of-Oneness *[tawḥīd]*—deserves the honor of admission to the sessions of the loving friends *[majālis al-aḥbāb]*. You must therefore extricate your own lower self *[nafs]*, O my brother, from the business of planning your life *[tadbīr]*. Do not take it upon yourself to manage that which Someone other than you will manage on your behalf. You must move beyond the characteristic features of your human nature *[bashariyya]*, beyond every attribute of character that is incompatible with your servitude *[ʿubūdiyya]*, so that you will always be ready to respond to the summons of the Lord of Truth, and will ever be near to His presence.

Stay close to the commanders *[āmirīn]*, for then you will be numbered among the people of the inner and of certainty *[ahl al-bāṭin wa 'l-yaqīn]*, and cling to the dust of the doorsteps *[aʿtāb]*, always cultivating good behavior *[ādāb]*, for then you will be numbered among the people of the outer and of faith *[ahl aẓ-ẓāhir wa 'l-īmān]*—at every moment, and at every station and degree, according to those who know by direct experience *[ʿārifīn]*. As he [Walī Raslān] (may Allāh be well pleased with him) has said:

"The people of the inner are with certainty, and the people of the outer are with faith. So when the heart of the master of certainty is

[74] ***idhā lam yabqa ʿalai-ka ḥaraka li-nafsi-ka, kamila yaqīnu-ka—wa idhā lam yabqa la-ka wujūd kamila tawḥīdu-ka.***

stimulated [in response to anything other than Allāh], his certainty is deficient, and when no notion ever occurs to him, his certainty is perfect. And when the heart of the master of faith is stimulated in response to anything other than the Divine command, his faith is defective, and when it is stirred by the Divine command, his faith is complete."[75]

That is to say, the people of the inner *[ahl al-bāṭin]* are with certainty *[yaqīn]*, due to their having attained to the degree of seeing with one's own eyes *[martabat al-ʿiyān]*, and because of their having entered the station of active goodness *[maqām al-iḥsān]*. As for the people of the outer *[ahl aẓ-ẓāhir]*, they are with faith *[īmān]*, due to their having attained to the degree of belief *[martabat at-taṣdīq]*, and because of their having entered the station of voluntary compliance *[maqām al-idhʿān]*. The latter grade constitutes a minor rank of sainthood *[wilāya ṣughrā]*, and it is absolutely necessary for the seeker to step up to its threshold during the initial stage of his spiritual journey. The former grade, on the other hand, constitutes a major rank of sainthood *[wilāya kubrā]*, a rank to which the seeker must inevitably attain at the ultimate stage of his spiritual progress.

The master of certainty *[ṣāḥib al-yaqīn]* is one of those who have advanced to the final stages of spiritual development *[ahl an-nihāyāt]*. When his heart becomes agitated, therefore, it must mean that his certainty is defective, since this is an unmistakable indication of his paying attention to that which is apart [from the Lord]. It is this distraction that causes him to exhibit signs of agitation. When not a single disturbing notion occurs to him, on the other hand, due to his total immersion in the fathomless depths of togetherness *[lujjat al-jamʿiyya]*, it must mean that his certainty is complete, since this is an unmistakable indication of his paying perfect attention [to the Lord], and a sure sign that he retains not a trace of interest in that which is apart [from Him].

[75] ***ahl al-bāṭin maʿa 'l-yaqīn—wa ahl aẓ-ẓāhir maʿa 'l-īmān—fa-matā taḥarraka qalb ṣāḥib al-yaqīn [li-ghairi 'llāh] naqaṣa yaqīnu-hu—wa matā lam yakhṭir la-hu khāṭir kamila yaqīnu-hu—wa matā taḥarraka qalb ṣāḥib al-īmān li-ghairi 'l-amri 'l-ilāhī, naqaṣa īmānu-hu—wa matā taḥarraka bi-'l-amri 'l-ilāhī, kamila īmānu-hu.*** (The words enclosed between brackets are missing from the text of al-Ḥamawī's commentary on the *Risāla*, although they do occur in the version quoted by Zakariyyāʾ al-Anṣārī.)

In the case of the master of faith *[ṣāḥib al-īmān]*, when his heart is stimulated in response to something other than the Divine command, and when he gets involved in whatever has distracted him, it must mean that his faith is defective, since this is an unmistakable indication of his being hopelessly adrift in the ocean of contradictions *[baḥr al-mukhālafāt]*. When his heart is stimulated by the Divine command, however, and he then proceeds to follow the courses of action we have outlined, it must mean that his faith is complete, since this clearly points to the fact that he is a slave *[mamlūk]* at the disposal of his Master *[Mawlā]*.

To put this subject in a nutshell, the following are the main points to be emphasized:

1. The people of the inner *[ahl al-bāṭin]* have attained to the station of active goodness *[maqām al-iḥsān]*, the station of one who worships Allāh as if he can see Him, and it is utterly absurd to suppose that anyone, while seeing Him, would also pay attention to something apart from Him. If someone is actually experiencing the direct vision [of Allāh], how can he possibly be affected by any ordinary impulse? How can he be held responsible for standing up or sitting down? If someone is drinking wine from these goblets, how can any disturbing notion possibly occur to him? How can the ear of his heart be expected to hear a ringing sound from that bell *[nāqūs]*?[76]

2. As for the people of the outer *[ahl aẓ-ẓāhir]*, they are standing by the doorway in the company of faith *[īmān]*, ready to hear and obey whatever may be required of them by the Book [of Allāh (Almighty and Glorious is He)] and the Sunna [of the Prophet (Allāh bless him and give him peace)]. They must not move from the spot, except to perform the duties they have been ordered to carry out. When they move into action for any other reason, it can only mean that their faith is defective. But when they move into action for this purpose alone, it means that their faith is complete, and that what they are seeking to gain from this station will be granted to them in full.

[76] The Arabic word *nāqūs* came to be applied to a bell, particularly the bell of a Christian church or convent. In the earliest days of Islām, however, it referred to a thin oblong piece of wood, which was beaten with a flexible rod called *wabīl*. This, rather than the bell, was used by the Christians of that time as an instrument for notifying the people of the times of prayer. Under the Greek name *simandro*, it was observed to be still in use in certain monasteries in the Levant during the first half of the nineteenth century. (See: Thomas Patrick Hughes, *Dictionary of Islam*, art. NĀQŪS.)

You must therefore be prepared, O my brother, to powder your cheeks with the dust of the doorsteps *[aʿtāb]*. You must comply with the [Divine] commandments and refrain from violating the [Divine] prohibitions, for then you may rest secure in the dwelling places of the loving friends *[aḥbāb]*. Once you have reached this point, your heart will be cleansed of everything apart [from the Lord] *[as-siwā]*. You will lose all interest in personal power and strength, and come to be one who casts himself down in prostration before the Master *[al-Mawlā]*. When you have attained to this station *[maqām]*, you will come to be numbered among those who are drawn near *[muqarrabīn]*, and you will be taken to task for things that are not held against ordinary believers *[muʾminīn]*. As he [Walī Raslān] (may Allāh be well pleased with him) has said:

"The sin of the people of certainty is unbelief, and the sin of the people of faith is falling short."[77]

That is to say, since the people of certainty *[ahl al-yaqīn]* have attained to the station of active goodness *[maqām al-iḥsān]*, they are not granted forgiveness for a simple lapse into error, because the standard in their case is the standard applicable to those who are at the station of seeing with one's own eyes *[maqām al-ʿiyān]*. A black spot on a black gown does not have the same effect as a black spot on a white gown, and this principle is equally relevant to the severity of punishments. As for the people of faith *[ahl al-īmān]*, they are accorded a degree of tolerance that is not accorded to the people of highly developed intuition *[ahl al-ʿirfān]*. This is why the sin of the former is classed as a shortcoming, on account of the remnants [of worldly attachment] they still have inside them, and which hinder them from attaining to the special status of the latter group.

You must therefore make a very serious effort, O my brother, to purge both your outer self *[ẓāhir]* and your inner being *[bāṭin]* of the filth of contradictions *[najāsat al-mukhālafāt]*, so that your ritual prayer *[ṣalāt]* may enter the sphere of the Reality *[al-Ḥaqīqa]*, and so that you may come to be numbered among the truly dutiful servants *[muttaqīn]*, the lovers [of the Truth] *[muḥibbīn]*, the people who have advanced to the final stages of spiritual development *[ahl an-nihāyāt]*. [As Walī Raslān (may Allāh be well pleased with him) has said]:

"The dutiful servant is diligent, and the lover is totally trusting,

[77] ***maʿṣiyat ahl al-yaqīn kufr—wa maʿṣiyat ahl al-īmān naqṣ.***

and he who knows by direct experience is calm and serene, and he who is found is lost. There is no rest for a dutiful servant, and no movement for a lover, and no resolve for one who knows by direct experience, and no being found for one who is lost."[78]

Let us now consider each of these eight points in turn:

1. The dutiful servant *[muttaqī]* is diligently engaged in service, always on the watch for guidance, strongly committed to his aspiration. As Allāh (Exalted is He) has said:

> And as for those who strive in Our cause, We shall surely guide them to Our paths. (29:69)[79]

This is why, as the saying goes: "When a person has a job to do, he does not have a place to sit."[80] Somebody once said: "This teaching is based on serious dedication and diligent exertion." The point is also very well expressed in the saying: "In proportion to the weary toil invested, the lofty benefits are earned *[tuksabu 'l-maʿālī]*. If a person wishes to reach the heights, he must spend the nights awake *[sahira 'l-layālī]*. He may be keen to find the Truth, but then his eye drops off to sleep, and he plunges deep into the ocean in the quest for pearls *[min ṭalabi 'l-laʾālī]*."

2. The lover *[muḥibb]* is totally reliant on his Master *[Mawlā]*—in all his affairs—because he is completely content with the knowledge that Allāh has about him, and so feels no need for anyone apart from Him. As a result, the focus of his attention never shifts toward anyone other than Him.

The All-Generous One *[al-Karīm]* will never disappoint the hopes of those who seek [from Him] the satisfaction of their needs. The petitioner has only to present his need—within his innermost being *[sirr]* and as a confidential secret *[najwā]*—to the Lord of All the Worlds *[Rabb al-ʿĀlamīn]*, speaking in the language of his state of being and his own peculiar idiom *[bi-lisān ḥālihi wa qālihi]*, and intoning this request both in the early morning hours and through the later times of day.

[78] ***al-muttaqī mujtahid wa 'l-muḥibb muttakil wa 'l-ʿārif sākin wa 'l-mawjūd mafqūd—lā sukūn li-muttaqin wa lā ḥaraka li-muḥibb wa lā ʿazm li-ʿārif wa lā wujūd li-mafqūd.***

[79] *wa 'lladhīna jāhadū fīnā la-nahdiyannahum subulanā.*

[80] *man takun lahu qawma lam takun lahu qaʿda.*

O You who can see what is tucked inside the hidden recesses of the human soul *[mā fi 'ḍ-ḍamīr]*—and can hear it, too! You are the One who has made provision for everything that will ever come to pass. O You to whom appeal is made in all misfortunes and calamities! O You to whom the complainers and the panic-stricken turn! O You who keep the treasure houses of Your kingdom stored in the one word, "Be! *[kun]*." Bestow Your grace and favor, for all goodness is entirely at Your disposal. What device can I resort to, apart from knocking at Your door? And if You should drive me away, which door could I knock at then? To whom could I appeal and call upon by name, if Your gracious favor were to be withheld from this poor supplicant of Yours? Far be it from Your noble generosity that You should ever disappoint a beggar! May the gifts be abundant and the presents copious!

3. The person who knows by direct experience *[ʿārif]* is calm and serene. The making of plans *[tadbīr]* is no longer any concern of his, and he has lost the self-willed desire to exert his own power and strength, so the entire universe is ready to serve him, and his blissful good fortune *[saʿāda]* is now complete.

This is why, as somebody once put it: "When a man gives up trying to plan his own life, he settles into the sphere of trustful delegation *[tafwīḍ]*. From this point on, all his requirements are brought to him in solemn procession *[zuffat ilaih]*, just as the bride is conducted to the bridegroom."

To quote another excellent saying: "When I saw the decree of destiny *[qaḍāʾ]* taking its course, indubitably and inexorably, I really and truly placed my trust in my Creator *[tawakkaltu ḥaqqan ʿalā Khāliqī]*, and I surrendered myself *[aslamtu nafsī]* of my own free will."

4. He who is found is lost *[al-mawjūd mafqūd]*. That is to say, he who is found in the realm of genuine existence *[mawjūd bi-'l-wujūd al-ḥaqīqī]* is lost in the sense of being missing from the realm of illusory existence *[mafqūd ʿani-'l-wujūd al-wahmī]*. He recognizes nothing as being in existence except his Master *[Mawlā]*, and he does not rely on anything apart from Him.

Provided you have fully understood these explanations, the remaining points can be dealt with more concisely:

5. There can be no rest for a dutiful servant *[muttaqī]*, because he is constantly engaged in diligent striving *[ijtihād]*.

6. There is no need for movement on the part of a lover *[muḥibb]*, because he is perfectly content with the knowledge that Allāh has about him, and because this reliance is quite sufficient to meet all his needs.

7. There is no question of resolve or decision-making *[ʿazm]* in the case of one who knows by direct experience *[ʿārif]*, because of his detachment from his own power and strength. When the seeker experiences this detachment to the fullest extent, he gains the object of his quest and enjoys his blissful good fortune.

8. There is no being found *[wujūd]* [in illusory existence] for one who is lost *[mafqūd]* [missing from that kind of existence], because of his separation from that rotten heap of dung *[dimna]*, and because of his having replaced aloofness *[ṣudūd]* with loving communion *[tawāṣul]*.

It is therefore incumbent upon you, O my brother, to change your attitude and redirect your aspiration, so that you may obtain some benefit from these spritual states. You must separate yourself from familiar habits and the standards of others, so that you will be worthy of love *[maḥabba]*, and will come to be numbered among the men of distinction. As he [Walī Raslān] (may Allāh be well pleased with him) has told us:

"Love is experienced only after certainty, and when the lover is sincere in his love, his heart must be empty of all that is apart from Him (Exalted is He). **And as long as it retains any trace of love for anything but Him, he must be lacking in love."**[81]

Certainty *[yaqīn]* is the firm conviction that there is no benefactor in existence *[lā muḥsin fi 'l-wujūd]* except Allāh. If someone really and truly holds this firm conviction, he will be granted the experience of love, and he will then devote himself to worshipful service at his Master's door *[iʿtakafa bi-bāb Mawlāhu]*. If a person is sincere in this kind of commitment, his heart must be devoid of everything apart from Him.

[81] ***mā taḥṣulu 'l-maḥabba illā baʿda 'l-yaqīn—wa 'l-muḥibb aṣ-ṣādiq fī ḥubbi-hi qad khalā qalbu-hu mimmā siwā-hu—wa mā dāmat ʿalai-hi baqiyyat maḥabba li-siwā-hu, fa-huwa nāqiṣ al-maḥabba.***

As long as someone retains the slightest trace of love for anything other than Him, he must be lacking in love and lying in whatever claim he makes. By the passion *[hawā]* he displays in the presence of a sensual temptation, or in reaction to the impact of a disaster, he can easily be distinguished from a true servant of his Lord.

It is therefore incumbent upon you, O my brother, to be keenly ambitious in aspiring to these degrees of spiritual progress. This means that you must cease to indulge in all forms of pleasurable enjoyment *[taladhdhudhāt]*, and that you must become extinct to your personal existence, for only then will you acquire the degrees of progress and gain access to the highest stations *[maqāmāt]*. [As Walī Raslān (may Allāh be well pleased with him) has told us]:

"One who takes delight in misfortune, co-exists therewith, and one who takes delight and rejoices in prosperity co-exists with it, so when He makes them extinct to them, the enjoyment of misfortune and prosperity departs."[82]

That is to say, when someone takes delight in misfortune *[balā᾿]*, due to the fact that he regards it as emanating from his Master *[Mawlā]*, that person is still existent *[mawjūd]*, because the survival of his sensory awareness is maintained by the experience of drinking from the cups of pure wine. In the case of someone who takes delight in prosperity *[na῾mā᾿]*, enjoying the opportunities it provides for indulging his faculties and his senses, that person is also existent *[mawjūd]*, for he is immersed in the station of separation *[maqām al-farq]* from his head to the soles of his feet. When someone becomes extinct to the entire universe *[faniya ῾ani 'l-akwān]*, however, he no longer feels the sensation of pleasurable enjoyment, and he enters into the station of active goodness *[maqām al-iḥsān]*. As he [Walī Raslān] (may Allāh be well pleased with him) has said [in the passage quoted immediately above]: "So when He makes them extinct, the enjoyment of misfortune and prosperity departs."

[82] ***man taladhdhadha bi-'l-balā᾿ fa-huwa ma῾a-hu mawjūd; wa man taladhdhadha wa fariḥa bi-'n-na῾mā᾿, fa-huwa ma῾a-hu mawjūd; fa-idhā afnā-hum ῾an-hum dhahaba 't-taladhdhudh bi-'l-balā᾿ wa 'n-na῾mā᾿.*** (As quoted by Zakariyyā᾿ al-Anṣārī, this passage from the *Risāla* includes the phrase: **"So when Allāh makes him extinct *[fa-idhā afnā-hu 'llāh]*,"** as opposed to: "So when He makes them extinct to them ***[fa-idhā afnā-hum ῾an-hum]***." Zakariyyā᾿ was well aware of the alternative reading—from another manuscript at his disposal—and he extends his commentary to cover both versions.)

You must therefore make a very serious effort, O my brother, to attain to extinction in Him *[al-fanāʾ fī-hi]*, for then you will gain access to the station of love *[maqām al-maḥabba]*, and its significant features and meaningful contents will become apparent to you.

[Walī Raslān (may Allāh be well pleased with him) goes on to explain]: **"As for the lover, his breath is wisdom, and as for the loved one, his breath is power."**[83]

That is to say, the breath of the lover *[muḥibb]*—his speech, in other words—is an expression of wisdom *[ḥikma]*, due to the fact that it issues from him while his heart is still under wraps—with the result that no one hears him, unless he can find a willing listener and can make that person understand what he has to say.

In the case of the loved one *[maḥbūb]*, on the other hand, his breath—his speech, in other words—is an expression of power *[qudra]*, which means that he never speaks about anything without being heard and understood. Nothing in the entire universe will ever contradict his command, due to the high esteem in which he is held [by his Lord], and because he has been invested [by Him] with the robe of honor that signifies [in the words of Allāh (Almighty and Glorious is He)]:

> I am his ears with which he hears, and his eyes with which he sees, and his tongue with which he speaks.[84]

He is also bedecked with the noble adornment that signifies [in the

[83] ***al-muḥibb anfāsu-hu ḥikma wa 'l-maḥbūb anfāsu-hu qudra.***

[84] *kuntu samʿa-hu 'lladhī yasmaʿu bi-hi; wa baṣara-hu 'lladhī yabṣuru bi-hi; wa lisāna-hu 'lladhī yanṭuqu bi-hi.*

These words of Allāh (Almighty and Glorious is He) have been transmitted to us by the Prophet (Allāh bless him and give him peace) in a well-known Divine Saying *[Ḥadīth Qudsī]*. Several versions have come down to us, including those noted by Shaikh ʿAbd al-Qādir al-Jīlānī (may Allāh be well pleased with him) in the following passage from the Sixth Discourse of *Revelations of the Unseen [Futūḥ al-Ghaib]* (pp. 17 and 18 of the translation published by Al-Baz):

> In a Sacred Tradition *[Ḥadīth Qudsī]* related by the blessed Prophet, Allāh (Exalted is He) says:
>
> > "My servant constantly approaches Me through supererogatory acts of worship until I love him, and when I love him, I become his ears with which he hears, his eyes with which he sees, his hands with which he holds, and his legs with which he walks." In another version, the wording is: "So through Me he hears, through Me he sees, and through Me he understands."

words addressed by Allāh (Exalted is He) to the Prophet (Allāh bless him and give him peace)]:

> And it was not you who did the throwing, when you threw [that handful of dust or sand in battle with the unbelieving foe], but Allāh did the throwing. (8:17)[85]

This is because, while he is still in the universe as far as his outer body *[ẓāhir]* is concerned, he is separated from it from the standpoint of his heart and soul *[janān]* and the innermost recesses of his being *[sarā'ir]*. It is therefore incumbent upon you, O my brother, to practice the formal acts of worship *['ibādāt]*, [for, as Walī Raslān (may Allāh be well pleased with him) has told us]:

"Formal acts of worship are for the compensations, and love is for the nearnesses.[86] [In the words of Allāh (Almighty and Glorious is He)]:[87] 'I have prepared for My righteous servants that which no eye has ever seen, of which no ear has ever heard, and which has never occurred to any human heart. When they wish for Me, I give them that which no eye has ever seen and of which no ear has ever heard.'"[88]

In other words, formal acts of worship are rewarded, and this is why they can be said to yield compensations *[mu'āwaḍāt]*. As for love *[maḥabba]*, it is an both an inclination *[mail]* and an annihilation *[fanā']*, and this explains why nearnesses *[qurubāt]* accrue from it.

The worshipper *['ābid]* is someone who is dedicated to a form of service *[khidma]* for the sake of the blissful reward he expects to receive in the Garden of Paradise. The lover *[muḥibb]*, on the other hand, is someone who has become extinct to all personal interests *[fānin 'ani 'l-aghrāḍ]*. He no longer has any aim or purpose except that his Master *[Mawlā]* should be well pleased with him. This means that the lover is actually a servant *['abd]* in the true sense of the term *['ala 'l-ḥaqīqa]*, and he has therefore earned the right *[istaḥaqqa]* to have it said concerning

[85] *wa mā ramaita idh ramaita wa lākinna 'llāha ramā.*

[86] ***al-'ibādāt li'l-mu'āwaḍāt wa 'l-maḥabba li'l-qurubāt.***

[87] At this point—as noted by Zakariyyā' al-Anṣārī—Walī Raslān (may Allāh be well pleased with him) quotes one Divine Saying *[Ḥadīth Qudsī]*: "When they wish for Me..." immediately after another: "I have prepared...."

[88] ***a'dadtu li-'ibādī 's-ṣāliḥīn mā lā 'ain ra'at wa lā udhn sami'at wa lā khaṭara 'alā qalb bashar—lammā arādūnī lī, a'ṭaitu-hum mā lā 'ain ra'at wa lā udhn sami'at.***

him—as it may appropriately be said concerning all those who follow this Spiritual Path *[Ṭarīqa]*:

> I have prepared for My righteous servants that which no eye has ever seen, of which no ear has ever heard, and which has never occurred to any human heart.[89]

[This Divine Saying (*Ḥadīth Qudsī*) is applicable to them] because they have devoted their intentions wholly and sincerely [to winning the good pleasure of their Lord], and they are no longer affected by dread of the Fire of Hell and desire for the Gardens of Paradise. This is why it is equally appropriate to cite that other saying of His with reference to their case, namely:

> When they wish for Me, I give them that which no eye has ever seen, and of which no ear has ever heard.[90]

By mentioning this second Divine Saying *[Ḥadīth Qudsī]* immediately after the one he has already cited, Walī Raslān (may Allāh be well pleased with him) is implicitly suggesting a comparison with the act of drinking a second draught of water immediately after the first, without pausing to catch one's breath *[ʿalal baʿda nahal]*. He is also indicating that the All-Generous One *[al-Karīm]* bestows His gracious favor upon them continuously, without interruption.

You must therefore rouse yourself and make haste, O my brother, if you to wish to get something to drink from these watering places. You must become extinct to your passion *[hawā]* and your self-willed desire *[irāda]*, for thus you may come to be a servant with undivided loyalty *[ʿabd ṣirf]*. You will then have access to all that is available to the perfect human being *[al-insān al-kāmil]*. [As Walī Raslān (may Allāh be well pleased with him) has told us]:

"When He has made you extinct to your passion by decree, and to your self-will through knowledge, you will become a servant with undivided loyalty, with neither passion nor will of your own. Then the veil will be lifted for your benefit, so that servitude will vanish away into Oneness, for the servant will be annihilated and the Lord (Almighty and Glorious is He) will remain."[91]

[89] See note 88 on p. 85 above.

[90] See note 88 on p. 85 above.

[91] ***idhā afnā-ka ʿan hawā-ka bi-'l-ḥukm—wa ʿan irādati-ka bi'l-ʿilm—taṣīru ʿabdan ṣirfan, lā hawā la-ka wa lā irāda—fa-ḥīna'idhin yukshafu la-ka—fa-taḍmaḥillu 'l-ʿubūdiyya fī 'l-waḥdāniyya—fa-yafnā wa yabqā 'r-Rabb (ʿazza wa jall).***

That is to say, when He has made you extinct to your passion *[hawā]* through compliance with the commandments and nonviolation of the prohibitions [prescribed by the Sacred Law]. As Allāh (Exalted is He) has told us:

> But as for him who feared to stand before his Lord, and forbade the lower self to follow passion, surely the Garden [of Paradise] will be his final place of rest. (79:40,41)[92]

As for the expression "and [when He has made you extinct] to your self-will *[irāda]* through knowledge *[ʿilm]*," this means that you must let your self-will pass away into His Will, so that you belong to Him in terms of reality *[ḥaqīqatan]* and to you in the sense of a borrowed loan *[ʿāriyatan]*.

Once you have moved away from passion *[hawā]* and self-will *[irāda]*, entered the station of servitude *[maqām al-ʿubūdiyya]*, and come to be a servant with undivided loyalty *[ʿabd ṣirf]*, you will no longer be influenced by passion and self-will. At this point, therefore, the veil will be lifted for your sake. You will be honorably admitted to the sessions of intimate nearness *[majālis al-qurb]*, and you will come to be counted as one of the loving friends *[aḥbāb]*. The radiant lights of the Reality *[anwār al-Ḥaqīqa]* will then shine upon you, taking you away from you and rendering you extinct to you. Thus servitude *[ʿubūdiyya]* will vanish away from you into Oneness *[waḥdāniyya]*, for the servant *[ʿabd]* undergoes annihilation as the inevitable consequence of abandoning his personal characteristics *[awṣāf]*, while the Lord remains. At this point the servant is enveloped by the greatest of all His gifts of grace, as indicated by His words (Exalted is He):

> And it was not you who did the throwing, when you threw [that handful of dust or sand in battle with the unbelieving foe], but Allāh did the throwing. (8:17)[93]

This is what actually accounts for the supernatural exploits *[khārāʾiq]* and marvelous feats *[ʿajāʾib]* apparently performed by the Prophets *[anbiyāʾ]* and the saints *[awliyāʾ]*—not that they ever attribute such wonders to any power or strength of their own—even though they are

[92] *wa ammā man khāfa maqāma Rabbi-hi wa naha 'n-nafsa ʿani 'l-hawā—fa-inna 'l-jannata hiya 'l-maʾwā.*

[93] *wa mā ramaita idh ramaita wa lākinna 'llāha ramā.*

at the ultimate stage of servitude, the very perfection of servitude. Stories about them in this context are well known, and their extraordinary experiences have been recorded in works of literature. If you need any further evidence, you have only to consider the words of the Prophet (Allāh bless him and give him peace), in which he reports the Divine Saying *[Ḥadīth Qudsī]*:

> My servant constantly draws near to Me through supererogatory acts of worship until I love him, and when I love him, I become his ears with which he hears, his eyes with which he sees, his tongue with which he speaks....[94]

If the seeker is ever to reach the stage where this will apply to him, he cannot afford to be unfamiliar with any aspect of the various procedures we have been discussing. You must therefore rouse yourself, O my brother, and pursue a lofty aspiration, for then you may catch a whiff of these delicate flavors! You must cast yourself down in prostration at the door, for then you may be invested with a robe of honor like those bestowed upon the ardent lovers *[ʿushshāq]*. This requires the persistent cultivation of modes of behavior in keeping with the Sacred Law *[ādāb ash-Sharīʿa]*, and that you confine yourself strictly within its rules and regulations. It requires you to practice studious seclusion *[iʿtikāf]* in the garden of academic knowledge *[ḥadīqat al-ʿilm]*, and to spend your moments of relaxation within your private quarters. If you follow this course, you will eventually enter the deep sea of direct knowledge *[maʿrifa]*, and then, once you are immersed in its contents, you will come to be counted as one of the people of dalliance and playful teasing *[ahl ad-dalāl]*—as indicated by his [Walī Raslān's] words (may Allāh be well pleased with him):

"The whole of the Sacred Law is constriction, and the whole of academic knowledge is expansion, and the whole of direct knowledge is dalliance and playful teasing."[95]

The whole of the Sacred Law *[Sharīʿa]* is indeed a form of constriction *[qabḍ]*—because it is all about rules and regulations *[ḥudūd]*, struggles

[94] *lā yazālu ʿabdī yaqrubu ilayya bi-'n-nawāfili ḥattā uḥibba-hu ; fa-idhā aḥbabtu-hu kuntu samʿa-hu 'lladhī yasmaʿu bi-hi ; wa baṣara-hu 'lladhī yabṣuru bi-hi ; wa lisāna-hu 'lladhī yanṭuqu bi-hi....* (See also note 50 on p. 65 above.)

[95] ***ash-sharīʿa kullu-hā qabḍ—wa 'l-ʿilm kullu-hu basṭ—wa 'l-maʿrifa kullu-hā dalāl.***

and conflicts that must be waged in opposition to the lower self *[nafs]* with all its passionate inclinations, and various forms of combat [against other hostile forces].

The whole of [academic] knowledge *[ʿilm]* is indeed a form of expansion *[basṭ]*—because it provides you with the explanations you need in order to make sense of commonly occurring and recurring phenomena *[ʿawāʾid]*, and because it demonstrates for your benefit the tremendous grace and favor [of the Creator]. Your lower self *[nafs]* is excited by it, and you feel cheerfully disposed to pay early morning visits to the mosques *[masājid]*. When someone acquires knowledge, He who is All-Knowing really speaks to that person. If someone discovers the tip of a tree that has its roots in the Garden of Paradise, even a tree so tall that it might take a hundred years to cover the length of it, how can he fail to embark upon the climb? How can he think of anything but spending every last breath in the effort to reach those blissful delights?

This only applies, of course, to someone whose aspiration is directed toward the quest for objects belonging to the created universe *[ṭalab al-akwān]*. So what can we say about someone whose aspiration is directed toward the higher aim of attaining to the station of active goodness *[maqām al-iḥsān]*? How great is the difference between someone whose aspiration is directed toward the maidens *[ḥūr]* and mansions *[quṣūr]* of Paradise, and someone whose aspiration is directed toward the removal of the veils *[sutūr]* that screen him from the Truth!

As far as direct knowledge *[maʿrifa]* is concerned, the whole of it is indeed dalliance and playful teasing *[dalāl]*, inasmuch as the veil is removed to let you discover your true value *[ḥaqīqat qadrika]*, if you are one of the people of loving communion *[ahl al-wiṣāl]*.[96]

[96] As an explanation of Walī Raslān's statement (may Allāh be well pleased with him) that the whole of intuitive knowledge *[maʿrifa]* is dalliance and playful teasing *[dalāl]*, this commentary by al-Ḥamawī may be considered somewhat cryptic. Perhaps he intended it as an illustration of playful teasing! Be that as it may, Zakariyyāʾ al-Anṣārī is much more clearly explicit in his commentary on this point: "...the servant dallies with his Lord as a husband dallies with his wife, as when she gives him a coquettish display of defiance, although she is not really opposing him at all. This is sheer generosity and gracious favor from Him (Exalted is He), not an incitement intended to provoke. The station of playful teasing is the place for happy relaxation in speech and behavior."

Shaikh Abu 'l-Ḥasan ash-Shādhilī[97] (may Allāh be well pleased with him) once said: "If the light of the disobedient believer *[nūr al-mu'min al-'āṣī]* were to shine forth, it would spread its radiance over everything between heaven above and the earth below." So how would it be, O my brother, with the light of the obedient believer *[nūr al-mu'min aṭ-ṭā'i']*, and how would it be with the light of one who knows by direct experience *[nūr al-'ārif]*?

We have an indication of this in the words of Allāh (Exalted is He):

> Successful indeed is he who causes it [his soul] to grow in purity, and a failure indeed is he who stunts its growth. (91:9,10)[98]

That is to say, [a failure indeed is he] who keeps it hidden in the darkness by his sinful acts of disobedience.

You must therefore make a very serious effort, O my brother, to let your light shine forth. This means that you must make the best possible use of every single moment of your life. You must turn your aspiration toward love *[maḥabba]*, until you cease to exist [in relation to your worldly attachments], and come to be one of the people of blissful good fortune *[ahl as-sa'āda]*. As he [Walī Raslān] (may Allāh be well pleased with him) has told us:

"Our method is love, not labor, and annihilation, not perpetuity. When you enter into work, you belong to you, and when you enter into love, you belong to Him [(Exalted is He)]**. The worshipper looks to his worship, while the lover looks to his love."**[99]

That is to say, the crucial point *[madār]* of our method—the point upon which it is hinged—is love *[maḥabba]*, not labor *['amal]*. It is centered on the direct experience of grace *[shuhūd al-minna]*, and on ceasing to exist in relation to service *[al-fanā' 'ani 'l-khidma]*—for such is the actual state of affairs where the people of perfection *[sha'n ahl*

[97] See note 8 on p. 41 above.

[98] *qad aflaḥa man zakkā-hā—wa qad khāba man dassā-hā.*

[99] ***ṭarīqu-nā maḥabba, lā 'amal, wa fanā', lā baqā'—idhā dakhalta fī 'l-'amal kunta la-ka—wa idhā dakhalata fī 'l-maḥabba kunta la-hu [(ta'āla)]—al-'ābid ra'ā li-'ibādati-hi—wa 'l-muḥibb ra'ā li-maḥabbati-hi.*** (The word *ta'ālā* [Exalted is He] is absent from the quotation provided here by al-Ḥamawī, although it does occur in the version cited by Zakariyyā' al-Anṣārī. In the latter version, it should also be noticed, the sentence beginning with *al-'ābid* [the worshipper] is preceded by the word *idh* [since].)

al-kamāl] are concerned. If you need further evidence of this, you have only to consider his [the Prophet's] words (Allāh bless him and give him peace):

> And my chief comfort [literally, the cooling of my eye] has been made to reside in the ritual prayer.[100]

He did not say: "[My chief comfort has been granted] as a reward for performing the ritual prayer *[bi-'ṣ-ṣalāt]*."

The Shaikh [Walī Raslān] (may Allāh be well pleased with him) has also drawn your attention to this, by saying: "When you enter into the work [of formal worship], you belong to you." In other words, when you enter into the work [of formal worship], regarding it as a source of benefit to yourself, and relying upon it [to yield such benefit], you belong to you. In conducting this transaction, that is to say, you are concentrating on your own lower self *[nafs]* and confirming its identity, inasmuch as you have attached importance to the work it can perform.

When you enter into love *[maḥabba]*, on the other hand, you belong to Him—because the lover *[muḥibb]* recognizes nothing in anything except his Master *[Mawlā]*, and he neither depends nor relies upon anyone apart from Him, for he is truly aware of the real meaning *[mutaḥaqqiq bi-ḥaqīqa]* of "There is no god but Allāh *[lā ilāha illa 'llāh]*." When someone is like this, he belongs to Allāh.

This explains why he [Walī Raslān (may Allāh be well pleased with him)] next goes on to say: "The worshipper looks to his worship *[al-ʿābid rāʾin li-ʿibādati-hi]*,"—in other words, he relies upon it entirely—"and the lover looks to his love *[al-muḥibb rāʾin li-maḥabbati-hi]*"—in other words, he attributes it to the gracious favor of his Master *[Mawlā]*, and this is why he is so keenly interested in everything that brings him in contact with it.

He [Walī Raslān (may Allāh be well pleased with him)] could have made his point more clearly if he had said: "The lover becomes extinct in his love *[al-muḥibb fānin fī maḥabbati-hi]*." Perhaps this alternative reading does in fact occur in some of the manuscripts that have not become available to us.

100 *wa juʿilat qurratu ʿainī fi 'ṣ-ṣalāt.*

You must therefore make a very serious effort, O my brother, if you are to be granted access to the station of love *[maqām al-maḥabba]*. Direct knowledge *[maʿrifa]* may then be bestowed upon you, and you may eventually attain to a major degree of sainthood *[wilāya]*.

[As Walī Raslān (may Allāh be well pleased with him) has told us]:

"When you have come to acknowledge Him, your breathing will be through Him, and your movements will belong to Him, but if you are ignorant of Him, your movements will be your own."[101]

That is to say, when you have come to acknowledge Him—through your personal experience *[bi-maʿrifati nafsi-ka]* of your own poverty, weakness, incompetence and insignificance—your every breath will be breathed on account of Him, for you will recognize the fact that affluence, strength, power and glory, all belong to Him alone. You must be acutely aware of your own human qualities, for then He will assist and support you with His qualities *[awṣāf]*. You must be acutely aware of your personal poverty, for then He will assist and support you with His boundless wealth. You must be acutely aware of your personal weakness, for then He will assist and support you with His might and His strength. You must be acutely aware of your personal insignificance, for then He will assist and support you with His glory. You must be acutely aware of your personal incompetence, for then He will assist and support you with His power.

If you are ignorant of Him—due to your dedicated pursuit of the interests of your own lower self *[nafs]*, and because of the great importance you attach to it and to the management of its affairs—it is indeed true to say that your movements belong to you, not to your Master *[Mawlā]*. As long as this is the case, you are far removed from the path you must follow in order to attain to your rank of honor and your status of nobility.

You must therefore rouse yourself, O my brother, and waste no time in adopting a lofty aspiration. You must detach yourself from your personal power and strength, for only then will you derive any benefit from these exalted degrees of spiritual progress. [As Walī Raslān (may Allāh be well pleased with him) has told us]:

"The formal worshipper has no rest; and the ascetic has no

[101] ***idhā ʿarafta-hu kānat anfāsu-ka bi-hi wa ḥarakātu-ka la-hu—wa idhā jahilta-hu kānat ḥarakātu-ka la-ka.***

appetite; and the champion of truth has no dependent reliance; and he who is endowed with direct knowledge has neither might nor strength, neither choice nor will, neither movement nor rest; and he who is existent has no existence."[102]

Let us now consider each of these points in turn:

1. The formal worshipper *[ʿābid]* has no rest *[sukūn]*—because he is constantly engaged in striving *[mujāhada]*.

2. The ascetic *[zāhid]* has no appetite *[raghba]*—because he is committed to abstaining from nonessential provisions *[zawāʾid]*, and has therefore confined himself to these [sparsely furnished] tables *[mawāʾid]*.

3. The champion of truth *[ṣiddīq]* has no dependent reliance *[irtikān]*—due to his having entered the station of active goodness *[maqām al-iḥsān]*.

4. He who is endowed with direct knowledge *[ʿārif]* has no personal power and strength *[ḥawl wa quwwa]*—because of his having attained to the station of seeing with one's own eyes *[maqām al-ʿiyān]*, and due to his having perfected the qualities of chivalry *[futuwwa]*. When someone has attained to this station, he feels too modest to assert his own choice or will in the presence of his Master's choice *[ikhtiyār]* and will *[irāda]*, and his sense of propriety refuses to let him become engaged—whether actively or passively—in the fulfillment of his personal needs.

5. He who is existent *[mawjūd]*—in the sense of enjoying the existence in perpetuity *[wujūd al-baqāʾ]* that comes in the wake of annihilation *[fanāʾ]*—has no existence [in the ordinary sense], due to the fact that he has now become extinct in relation to his illusory existence *[wujūd wahmī]*.

You must also be sure to learn the lessons taught at the station of hereditary transmission *[maqām al-wirātha]*, for this represents a straight and unbroken line connecting all the centuries. It is therefore incumbent upon you, O my brother, to enter the station of following [in the footsteps of those who have paved the way] *[maqām al-mutābaʿa]*, for

[102] ***al-ʿābid mā la-hu sukūn—wa 'z-zāhid mā la-hu raghba—wa 'ṣ-ṣiddīq mā la-hu irtikān—wa ʿārif mā la-hu ḥawl wa lā quwwa wa lā ikhtiyār wa lā irāda wa lā ḥaraka wa lā sukūn—wa 'l-mawjūd mā la-hu wujūd.***

then you may be able to traverse these various stages of spiritual progress. You will thus become estranged from you, and so be granted intimate friendship *[uns]* with Him. [As Walī Raslān (may Allāh be well pleased with him) has told us]:

"When you have come to be on familiar terms with Him, you will be estranged from you."[103]

The enjoyment of intimate friendship with Him (Exalted is He) is a privilege that will be granted only after separation from all others. Your own self *[nafsu-ka]* counts as an "other," and this explains why preoccupation with it is one of the factors that condemn you to loneliness, and which threaten to expose you to that scorching Fire of Hell. You must therefore turn your back upon this lower world, and adopt a genuine intention to embark upon the journey here described, for such an intention represents your speediest means of transport. This is what he [Walī Raslān] (may Allāh be well pleased with him) was alluding to when he said [quoting words attributed to Allāh (Exalted is He)]:

"'If someone is preoccupied with Us for his own sake, we shall make him blind. But if someone is preoccupied with Us for Our sake, We shall give him sight.'"[104]

That is to say: "If someone is preoccupied with serving Us for the sake of the benefits that will accrue to himself, We shall keep him at a distance and We shall make him blind. But if someone is preoccupied with Us for the sole purpose of gaining access to Our presence, We shall draw him close and enable him to see."

This means, O my brother, that you must not direct your aspiration toward anything other than Him, for such an intention would be no more useful—as a means of transport—than the miller's donkey set loose from the mill. You must also consider his [the Prophet's] words (Allāh bless him and give him peace):

> Actions derive their value from the intentions [on the strength of which they are performed], and every man is entitled to what he has intended. So, if someone's migration is [intended to take him] to Allāh and His Messenger, his migration will be [accepted as being] toward Allāh and

[103] ***idhā 'sta'nasta bi-hi istawḥashta min-ka.***

[104] ***man ishtaghala bi-nā la-hu a'mainā-hu—wa man ishtaghala bi-nā la-nā baṣṣarnā-hu.***

His Messenger. But if someone's migration is [intended to take him] to some worldly fortune, or to a woman he proposes to marry, his migration will be to whatever he has migrated toward.[105]

You must contemplate this statement, O my brother, with the eye of perceptive insight *[ʿain al-baṣīra]*, for it will help you to see beyond your passionate inclinations *[hawā]*. It will enable you to discover the Reality *[Ḥaqīqa]*, at which point you will truly experience the desired goal. As he [Walī Raslān] (may Allāh be well pleased with him) has told us:

"When your passion has faded away, the door of the Reality will be unveiled for your benefit, so that your own will is annihilated and Oneness is unveiled to you. [And then you will realize] that it is He, not you."[106]

That is to say, once He has enabled you to see beyond your passionate inclinations *[hawā]*—by bringing your lower self *[nafs]* to the point of acknowledging that its state is one of poverty, weakness, incompetence and insignificance—you will then come to acknowledge your Lord as the One who possesses all wealth, all strength, all power, and all glory.

The door of the Reality *[al-Ḥaqīqa]* will then be unveiled for your benefit, and your own actions *[afʿāl]* will thereupon fade away into His actions, your own characteristics *[awṣāf]* into His characteristics, and your own essence *[dhāt]* into His essence. As your self-will *[irāda]* becomes extinct, so will your interest in making personal choices *[ikhtiyār]* and in planning your own future *[tadbīr]*. You will recognize through your own direct experience that there is One, and no one else apart from Him, who can actually bring about the fulfillment of wishes and choices and plans. You will acknowledge that He is the One in control *[Huwa 'l-Mutaṣarrif]* of all situations, not you.

[105] *innama 'l-aʿamālu bi-'n-niyyati wa innamā li-kulli 'mriʾin bi-mā nawā—fa-man kānat hijratu-hu ila 'llāhi wa Rasūlihi fa-hijratu-hu ila llāhi wa Rasūlihi wa man kānat hijratu-hu ilā dunyā yuṣību-hā awi 'mratin yatazawwaju-hā fa-hijratu-hu ilā mā hājara ilaih.*

[106] ***idhā zāla hawā-ka kushifa la-ka ʿan bāb al-ḥaqīqa—fa-tafnā irādatu-ka fa-yukshafu la-ka ʿani 'l-waḥdāniyya—[fa-tuḥaqqiqu] anna-hu Huwa lā anta.*** (The words ***fa-tuḥaqqiqu*** **[and then you will realize]** are missing from this quotation as it is given here in the text of al-Ḥamawī's commentary—probably because of a scribal error—although they do occur in the version cited by Zakariyyāʾ al-Anṣārī. It is also worth noting that Zakariyyāʾ prefers the reading: **"And then you will realize that it is He in us *[anna-hu Huwa bi-nā]*,"** although he does inform us that one manuscript copy reads: **"...that it is He, not you *[anna-hu Huwa lā anta]*."**

You will therefore dismount and settle down within His sanctuary. You will find shelter inside His guesthouse and in the reality of "There is no god but Allāh *[lā ilāha illa 'llāh]*." You will also enjoy the secure protection of "There is no power and no strength except through Allāh *[lā ḥawla wa lā quwwata illa bi-'llāh]*." Your drinking fountain will be trustful delegation *[tafwīḍ]* and resignation *[taslīm]*, and goblets of this nectar will be passed around to you—enough to give you a taste of the blissful delight of nearness [to the Lord]. Such blissful happiness is indeed attainable, for, as he [Walī Raslān] (may Allāh be well pleased with him) has told us:

"If you surrender to Him, He will draw you close, but if you argue with Him, He will keep you at a distance."[107]

That is to say, if you surrender to Him, He will draw you close—on account of your genuine commitment *[taḥaqquq]* at that earlier stage, when you were at the station of servitude *[maqām al-ʿubūdiyya]*. But if you argue with Him, He will keep you at a distance—on account of your obstinate refusal to accept the decrees of Lordship *[aḥkām ar-rubūbiyya]*.

You must therefore adopt an attitude of submissiveness and humility in the presence of your Master *[Mawlā]*. You must draw close to Him through Him, instead of trying to approach Him by means of your own lower self *[nafs]*, for only then will you attain to your lofty goal. [As Walī Raslān (may Allāh be well pleased with him) has told us]:

"If you draw near through Him, He will bring you close, but if you draw near through you, He will keep you at a distance."[108]

To you through you, dear sirs, I have come to you, so do not refuse to notice one who has been guilty of bad manners! I count on you to say: "May Allāh pardon what has happened in the past"—for gracious kindness on your part is far from extraordinary.

[Walī Raslān (may Allāh be well pleased with him) goes on to say]:

"If you seek Him for your own sake, He will burden you"—on account of your attachment to your personal interests—**"But if you seek Him for His sake, He will pamper you"**[109]—on account of your detachment from your personal interests.

[107] ***in sallamta ilai-hi qarraba-ka—wa in nāzaʿta-hu abʿada-ka.***

[108] ***in taqarrabta bi-hi qarraba-ka—wa in taqarrabta bi-ka abʿada-ka.***

[109] ***in ṭalabta-hu la-ka kallafa-ka—wa in ṭalabta-hu la-hu dallala-ka.***

["Your nearness to Him is your separation from you, while your distance is your sticking with you."][110]

"If you come without you, He will accept you"—on account of your genuine commitment to the station of the realization-and-affirmation-of-Oneness *[maqām at-tawḥīd]*. **"But if you come through you, He will exclude you"**[111]—that is to say, He will exclude you on account of your ill-mannered behavior, the fact that you are guilty of having associated partners with Him *[shirk]*, and your failure to meet the requirements of the station of singular devotion *[maqām at-tafrīd]*.

"The worker is hardly likely to be free of attachment to his labor"—due to the fact that the dust of polytheistic association *[shirk]* continues to cling to him. **"So be one of the sort disposed towards grace, not one of the sort disposed towards work"**[112]—in order that you may be granted access to the drinking fountain of the realization-and-affirmation-of-Oneness *[mashrab at-tawḥīd]*, and so that the goblets holding its contents may be passed around to you.

"If you know Him, you will come to rest"—in His presence, on account of your genuine acknowledgment of the fact that there can be no salvation except through abject prostration before Him. **"But if you are ignorant of Him, you will be agitated"**—on account of your polytheistic association *[shirk]* and your sense of disappointment. This is why the limbs and organs of the physical body are also affected by your spiritual state. **"So the point is that He should be and you should not be."**[113]

This station *[maqām]* will be fully accessible to you, once you have really experienced annihilation *[fanā']*, once you have come to be numbered among the men of distinction *[rijāl]*, once you have drunk the juice of direct knowledge *[ma'rifa]*, and when the cups of the people of perfection *[ahl al-kamāl]* have been handed around to you.

110 ***[qurbu-ka ilai-hi khurūju-ka min-ka—wa bu'du-ka wuqūfu-ka ma'a-ka.]*** (This sentence is missing from the text of al-Ḥamawī's commentary, although it does occur in the version of the *Risāla* discussed by Zakariyyā' al-Anṣārī.)

111 ***in ji'ta bi-lā anta qabila-ka—wa in ji'ta bi-ka ḥajaba-ka.***

112 ***al-'āmil lā yakādu yakhluṣu min ru'yat 'amali-hi—fa-kun min qabīl al-minna—lā min qabīl al-'amal.***

113 ***in 'arafta-hu sakanta—wa in jahilta-hu taḥarrakta—fa-'l-murād an yakūna Huwa wa lā takūna anta.***

You must therefore rouse yourself, O tenderhearted brother, and set out in pursuit of a lofty aspiration. You must forge ahead and leave the common folk *[ʿawāmm]* behind, for then you may reach the pools and basins of the élite *[khawāṣṣ]*—or even the élite of the élite *[khawāṣṣ al-khawāṣṣ]*—and bathe your feet therein. Blissful good fortune will then be yours to enjoy for all eternity.

"As for the common folk, their works are [suspect, and as for the élite, their works are] good deeds, [and as for the élite of the élite, their works are degrees of spiritual progress]"[114]—on account of their ability to recognize true value, their contrite humility in the station of the realization-and-affirmation-of-Oneness *[maqām at-tawḥīd]*, and their abandonment of all that deserves to be regarded with suspicion.

"Whenever you shun your passion, your faith is reinforced"[115]—on account of your healthy freedom from unruly contradictions. **"And whenever you shun your own essence, your realization-and-affirmation-of-Oneness is reinforced"**[116]—on account of your being extinct in relation to you *[li-fanāʾi-ka ʿan-ka]*, and your total immersion in all forms of dutiful compliance *[muwāfaqāt]*.

Well then, my dear friend and brother, if you wish to see a goblet of this nectar being handed around to you, you must draw close to your Master *[Mawlā]* with the whole of you, and you must shun all else apart from Him. [As Walī Raslān (may Allāh be well pleased with him) has told us]:

"Creatures are a screen and you are a screen, but the Lord of Truth is not one to be secluded"[117]—since, if anything were to try and screen Him, He would cover it; and if He covered it, He would be Present *[Ḥāḍir]* to it; and if He were Present to it, He would be Prevailing over it, for He is Ever-Prevailing *[Qāhir]* over His servants.

[114] ***al-ʿawāmm aʿmālu-hum [muttahamāt—wa 'l-khawāṣṣ aʿamālu-hum] qurubāt—[wa khawāṣṣ al-khawāṣṣ aʿamālu-hum darajāt.]*** (The words enclosed between brackets are all missing from the text of al-Ḥamawī's commentary—almost certainly due to scribal error—although they do occur in the version of the *Risāla* recorded by Zakariyyāʾ al-Anṣārī.)

[115] ***kullamā ijtanabta hawā-ka qawiya īmānu-ka.***

[116] ***wa kullamā ijtanabta dhāta-ka qawiya tawḥīdu-ka.***

[117] ***al-khalq ḥijāb wa anta ḥijāb wa 'l-Ḥaqq laisa bi-maḥjūb.*** (In the version of the Risāla cited by Zakariyyāʾ al-Anṣārī, this sentence is followed by: **"It is He who conceals Himself *[wa Huwa yaḥtajibu]*."**)

"And He is concealed from you because of you"[118]—that is to say, because of your preoccupation with your own lower self *[nafs]*, for you would otherwise be aware that He is actually closer to you than your jugular vein *[ḥabl al-warīd]*.[119]

"And you are concealed from you because of you"[120]—if you are sincere in making your approach to Him, so that you become extinct [in relation to you], and cast yourself down in abject prostration before Him.

"So separate from you—that is to say, abandon all attachment to your personal characteristics *[awṣāf]*—**"and you shall witness Him."**[121]

This means that you are about to enter the station of active goodness *[maqām al-iḥsān]*, and that you must therefore refrain from indulging all those personal inclinations of yours, as indicated by his [the Prophet's] words (Allāh bless him and give him peace):

> Pay careful attention to Allāh and He will take good care of you. Pay careful attention to Allāh and you will find Him face to face with you. If you have a request to make, you must put your request to Allāh, and if you need to ask for help, you must ask for help from Allāh.[122]

If you need help, O my brother, in order to achieve these goals, you must therefore seek that help from no one but your Master *[Mawlā]*. To

[118] ***wa Huwa maḥjūb ʿan-ka bi-ka.*** (In the version of the *Risāla* cited by Zakariyyāʾ al-Anṣārī, this sentence reads: "**It is He who conceals Himself... *[wa Huwa yaḥtajibu]*....**")

[119] An allusion to the verse *[āya]* of the Qurʾān in which Allāh (Almighty and Glorious is He) has told us:

> We have indeed created man...and We are nearer to him than the jugular vein *[wa la-qad khalaqna 'l-insāna...wa Naḥnu aqrabu ilai-hi min ḥabli 'l-warīd]*. (50:16)

[120] ***wa anta maḥjūb ʿan-ka bi-ka.*** (In the version of the *Risāla* cited by Zakariyyāʾ al-Anṣārī, this sentence reads: "**And you are secluded from you because of Him *[wa anta muḥtajib ʿan-ka bi-hi]*.**" Zakariyyāʾ does mention that one manuscript has "**because of them *[bi-him]***"—that is, because of creatures—but he was apparently unaware of the reading given here.)

[121] ***fa-'nfaṣil ʿan-ka tashhad-hu.*** (In the version of the *Risāla* cited by Zakariyyāʾ al-Anṣārī, this sentence ends with the verb ***tashhad*** **[and you shall witness]**—without the object-pronoun ***-hu*** **[Him]**. Zakariyyāʾ assumes the implied object to be "all the blessings and generous favor He has graciously bestowed upon you.")

[122] *iḥfaẓi 'llāha yaḥfaẓ-ka: iḥfaẓi 'llāha tajid-hu tujāha-ka—wa idhā saʾalta fa 'sʾali 'llāh—wa idha 'staʿanta fa-'staʿin bi-'llāh.*

recognize the truth of this, you have only to recall His words (Exalted is He):

> You alone do we worship, and to You alone do we pray for help. (1:4)[123]

You will thus become worthy to receive your rank of honor and your status of nobility.

Praise be to Allāh *[al-ḥamdu li'llāhi]* in each and every situation *[ʿalā kulli ḥāl]*. Blessings and peace be upon him [the Prophet] who set the example to be followed by the masters of perfection *[arbāb al-kamāl]*—and upon his family and all his Companions *[Aṣḥābi-hi]*—for he has shown you the way that leads to his Master, and to prostration at His door *[ʿalā bābi-hi]*.

Praise be to Allāh, Lord of All the Worlds
[al-ḥamdu li'llāhi Rabbi 'l-ʿālamīn].

Āmīn.

(The transcription of the text of this book, containing the Commentary *[Sharḥ]* entitled *The Inspiration of the All-Merciful [Fatḥ ar-Raḥmān]* has now been completed—on Tuesday, the fifth day of the month of Ṣafar in the year 1307 of the Prophetic Hijra.)

123 *iyyāka naʿbudu wa iyyāka nastaʿīn*.

About the Translator

Muhtar Holland was born in 1935, in the ancient city of Durham in the North East of England. This statement may be considered anachronistic, however, since he did not bear the name Muhtar until 1969, when he was moved—by powerful experiences in the *latihan kejiwaan* of Subud—to embrace the religion of Islām.*

At the age of four, according to an entry in his father's diary, he said to a man who asked his name: "I'm a stranger to myself." During his years at school, he was drawn most strongly to the study of languages, which seemed to offer signposts to guide the stranger on his "Journey Home," apart from their practical usefulness to one who loved to spend his vacations traveling—at first on a bicycle—through foreign lands. Serious courses in Latin, Greek, French, Spanish and Danish, with additional smatterings of Anglo-Saxon, Italian, German and Dutch. Travels in France, Germany, Belgium, Holland and Denmark. Then a State Scholarship and up to Balliol College, Oxford, for a degree course centered on the study of Arabic and Turkish. Travels in Turkey and Syria. Then National Service in the Royal Navy, with most of the two years spent on an intensive course in the Russian language.

In the years since graduation from Oxford and Her Majesty's Senior Service, Mr. Holland has held academic posts at the University of Toronto, Canada; at the School of Oriental and African Studies in the University of London, England (with a five-month leave to study Islamic Law in Cairo, Egypt); and at the Universiti Kebangsaan in Kuala Lumpur, Malaysia (followed by a six-month sojourn in Indonesia). He also worked as Senior Research Fellow at the Islamic Foundation in Leicester, England, and as Director of the Nūr al-Islām Translation Center in Valley Cottage, New York.

* The name Muhtar was received at that time from Bapak Muhammad Subuh Sumohadiwidjojo, of Wisma Subud, Jakarta, in response to a request for a suitable Muslim name. In strict academic transliteration from the Arabic, the spelling would be *Mukhtār*. The form *Muchtar* is probably more common in Indonesia than *Muhtar*, which happens to coincide with the modern Turkish spelling of the name.

His freelance activities have mostly been devoted to writing and translating in various parts of the world, including Scotland and California. He made his Pilgrimage *[Ḥajj]* to Mecca in 1980.

Published works include the following:

Al-Ghazālī. *On the Duties of Brotherhood.* Translated from the Classical Arabic by Muhtar Holland. London: Latimer New Dimensions, 1975. New York: Overlook Press, 1977. Repr. 1980 and 1993.

Sheikh Muzaffer Ozak al-Jerrahi. *The Unveiling of Love.* Translated from the Turkish by Muhtar Holland. New York: Inner Traditions, 1981. Westport, Ct.: Pir Publications, 1990.

Ibn Taymīya. *Public Duties in Islām.* Translated from the Arabic by Muhtar Holland. Leicester, England: Islamic Foundation, 1982.

Hasan Shushud. *Masters of Wisdom of Central Asia.* Translated from the Turkish by Muhtar Holland. Ellingstring, England: Coombe Springs Press, 1983.

Al-Ghazālī. *Inner Dimensions of Islamic Worship.* Translated from the Arabic by Muhtar Holland. Leicester, England: Islamic Foundation, 1983.

Sheikh Muzaffer Ozak al-Jerrahi. *Irshād.* Translated [from the Turkish] with an Introduction by Muhtar Holland. Warwick, New York: Amity House, 1988. Westport, Ct.: Pir Publications, 1990.

Sheikh Muzaffer Ozak al-Jerrahi. *Blessed Virgin Mary.* Translation from the original Turkish by Muhtar Holland. Westport, Ct.: Pir Publications, 1991.

Sheikh Muzaffer Ozak al-Jerrahi. *The Garden of Dervishes.* Translation from the original Turkish by Muhtar Holland. Westport, Ct.: Pir Publications, 1991.

Sheikh Muzaffer Ozak al-Jerrahi. *Adornment of Hearts.* Translation from the original Turkish by Muhtar Holland and Sixtina Friedrich. Westport, Ct.: Pir Publications, 1991.

Sheikh Muzaffer Ozak al-Jerrahi. *Ashki's Divan.* Translation from the Original Turkish by Muhtar Holland and Sixtina Friedrich. Westport, Ct.: Pir Publications, 1991.

Shaikh ʿAbd al-Qādir al-Jīlānī. *Revelations of the Unseen (Futūḥ al-Ghaib).* Translated from the Arabic by Muhtar Holland. Houston, Texas: Al-Baz Publishing, Inc., 1992

Shaikh ʿAbd al-Qādir al-Jīlānī. *The Sublime Revelation (al-Fatḥ ar-Rabbānī).* Translated from the Arabic by Muhtar Holland. Houston, Texas: Al-Baz Publishing, Inc., 1992

Shaikh ʿAbd al-Qādir al-Jīlānī. *Utterances (Malfūẓāt).* Translated from the Arabic by Muhtar Holland. Houston, Texas: Al-Baz Publishing, Inc., 1992

Shaikh ʿAbd al-Qādir al-Jīlānī. *The Removal of Cares (Jalāʾ al-Khawāṭir).* Translated from the Arabic by Muhtar Holland. Ft. Lauderdale, Florida: Al-Baz Publishing, Inc., 1997

Shaikh ʿAbd al-Qādir al-Jīlānī. *Sufficient Provision for Seekers of the Path of Truth (Al-Ghunya li-Ṭālibī Ṭariq al-Ḥaqq).* Translated from the Arabic (in 5 vols.) by Muhtar Holland. Hollywood, Florida: Al-Baz Publishing, Inc., 1997.

Shaikh ʿAbd al-Qādir al-Jīlānī. *Fifteen Letters (Khamsatta ʿAshara Maktuban).* Translated from the Arabic by Muhtar Holland. Hollywood, Florida: Al-Baz Publishing, Inc., 1997

BOOKS PUBLISHED BY AL-BAZ PUBLISHING INCLUDE:

1. **Revelations of the Unseen** (*Futūḥ al-Ghaib*) $20.00
   78 Discourses by Shaikh ʿAbd al-Qādir al-Jīlānī

2. **The Sublime Revelation** (*Al-Fatḥ ar-Rabbānī*) $29.00
   62 Discourses by Shaikh ʿAbd al-Qādir al-Jīlānī

3. **Utterances of Shaikh ʿAbd al-Qādir** (*Malfūẓāt*) $18.00

4. **The Removal of Cares** (*Jalāʾ al-Khawāṭir*) $25.00
   45 Discourses by Shaikh ʿAbd al-Qādir al-Jīlānī

5. **Sufficient Provision for Seekers of the Path of Truth**
   (*Al-Ghunya li-Ṭālibī Ṭarīq al-Ḥaqq*) $125.00 Set
   by Shaikh ʿAbd al-Qādir al-Jīlānī (may Allāh be well pleased with him)
   This encyclopedic work is a complete resource on the inner and outer aspects of Islām. The translation has been published in 5 volumes. 1738 pages. Translated by Muhtar Holland.

6. **Fifteen Letters** $12.00
   (*Khamsata ʿAshara Maktūban* otherwise known as *Maktūbāt*)
   Fifteen letters by Shaikh ʿAbd al-Qādir al-Jīlānī to one of his disciples. Originally written in Persian, they were translated into Arabic by ʿAlī Ḥusāmu'd-dīn al-Muttaqī (the Devout), who said of them, "... these letters comprise nuggets of wisdom and spiritual counsel, couched in various forms of allegory, metaphor, paraphrase and quotation, including approximately two hundred and seventy-five Qurʾānic verses. They also contain allusions to the experiences *[adhwāq]* and spiritual states *[ḥālāt]* of the Ṣūfis (may Allāh's good pleasure be conferred upon them all). Translated by Muhtar Holland.

7. **Concerning the Affirmation of Divine Oneness** $15.00
   (*Risālat at-Tawḥīd*)
   by Shaikh Walī Raslān ad-Dimashqī (d. A.H. 540)
   This is a Risāla on *shirk khafī* (hidden *shirk*). *Shirk* is associating partners with Allāh. Also in the book is a commentary by Shaikh Zakariyyāʾ al-Anṣārī (d. A.H. 926) called "*Kitāb Fatḥ ar-Raḥmān*." Also in the book is a commentary by Shaikh ʿAlī ibn ʿAṭiyya ʿAlawān al-Ḥamawī (d. A.H. 936) called "*Sharḥ Fatḥ ar-Raḥmān*." This is a very important book. Translated by Muhtar Holland.

8. **The Proper Conduct of Marriage in Islām** $18.00
by Imām al-Ghazālī
This is Book 12 of *Iḥyā ʿUlūm ad-Dīn*. Translated by Muhtar Holland.

9.. **The Most Beautiful Names of God** (*Al-Asmāʾ al-Ḥusnā*)
by Jamāʿa Majhūla $12.50
A chanted recital of the 99 Names of Allāh. Audio tape and CD.

10. **Necklaces of Gems** (*Qalāʾid al-Jawāhir*) $29.95
by Shaikh Muḥammad ibn Yaḥyā at-Tādifī
A Biography of Shaikh ʿAbd al-Qādir al-Jīlānī (may Allāh be well pleased with him), on the Marvelous Exploits of the Crown of the Saints, the Treasure-trove of the Pure, the Sulṭān of the *Awliyāʾ*, the Sublime *Quṭb*, Shaikh Muḥyi'd-dīn ʿAbd al-Qādir al-Jīlānī. Translated by Muhtar Holland.

11. **Emanations of Lordly Grace** (*al-Fuyūḍāt ar-Rabbāniyya*)
by Ismāʿīl Muḥammad Saʿīd al-Qādirī $29.00
A collection of the work and explanations of Shaikh ʿAbd al-Qādir al-Jīlānī (may Allāh be well pleased with him), that includes definition and attributes of the seven selves *[nafs]*, an explanation of the names of the seven stations *[maqāmāt]*, the creed *[ʿaqīda]* of the Supreme Helper (may Allāh be well pleased with him), the meaning of the names of the Qādiriyya order, the remarkable virtues of al-Jīlānī the *Quṭb*, the names of our master, ʿAbd al-Qādir, litanies *[awrād]* for the taming of hearts and for emergency situations; how to offer the greeting of peace *[salām]*to the men of the unseen *[Ghaib]* and much much more. Translated by Muhtar Holland.

For further titles please visit our web site at **www.albaz.com**

Orders or enquiries, or to be placed on our mailing list, contact:

Al-Baz Publishing, Inc.
1516 NE 38th Street
Oakland Park, Florida 33334

Phone: (425) 891-5444
E-mail: albaz@bellsouth.net